# STAFFORDSHIRE

*of one hundred years ago*

A FAMILY WALK

FAIRGROUND, LICHFIELD

# STAFFORDSHIRE

*of one hundred years ago*

## DAVID BUXTON

ALAN SUTTON

First published in the United Kingdom in 1993 by
Alan Sutton Publishing Ltd · Phoenix Mill · Stroud · Gloucestershire

First published in the United States of America in 1994 by
Alan Sutton Publishing Inc · 83, Washington Street · Dover · NH 03820

British Library Cataloguing in Publication Data

Buxton, David
Staffordshire of one hundred years ago
I. Title
942.46081

ISBN 0–7509–0419–4

BASS'S TRIP, BURTON ON TRENT

Typeset in 11/13 Bembo
Typesetting and origination by
Alan Sutton Publishing Limited.
Printed in Great Britain by
The Bath Press, Bath, Avon.

# Preface

In *Staffordshire of one hundred years ago* I have tried to recreate some of the feel and flavour of the late nineteenth and early twentieth centuries in Staffordshire. Old photographs provide the visual images of the period, the streets, factories and schools and, of greatest interest to most of us, the people who inhabited them. It is always fascinating to see how our ancestors looked as they went about their daily round. Everyone seems to be more formally dressed than most people are today. Working men wore hats, suits and ties to the factory and children were turned out in heavy layers of clothing that, to our eyes, seem totally unsuitable for play. If you didn't have a washing-machine would you send your young daughter out to play every day in a lacy white dress with several layers of petticoats and wearing a large hat? Where on earth did these people store their clothes? Women's clothes, particularly, were very bulky and one can't imagine storing more than one of those late Victorian dresses in a modern wardrobe. As for all the hats . . .

I have attempted to add to the interest of the photographs by placing alongside them extracts from contemporary writing on Staffordshire. Thus the text of the book is made up of short pieces taken from reminiscences, biographies, letters, short stories and newscuttings, all written in or about Staffordshire at the time of the photographs. Sometimes the extracts describe events or places that link up specifically with the adjacent pictures so that, for example, a story from a named village sits next to a contemporary picture of the village. Sometimes the appropriateness of the matching is a little more fanciful.

Most of the photographs and texts chosen for the book date from the 1880s to just after the turn of the century and although some stray a few years outside these limits I have included them if I believed they made a useful contribution and were still typical of the late nineteenth-century period. Although I have not attempted to include every town, village and community in the county I have tried to make the spread as geographically wide as possible and I hope that most areas are fairly represented. As this book describes Staffordshire of a

STRAWING AND PACKING CHINA

1

WOLVERHAMPTON WORKHOUSE

SAMUEL PEPLOE WOOD, GREAT HAYWOOD

century ago, I have included all areas that were within the old historic county boundaries of that time and so the change of boundary that moved most of the Black Country into a new county of West Midlands in 1974 is disregarded here.

I have added only short captions to the photographs, usually sufficient to simply locate the scene, but fuller details, where available, are listed along with the dates and sources at the end of the book. Text sources are also listed so that it will be possible to trace and read in full a piece that has whetted the appetite for more.

Assembling the material for this book has given me a great deal of pleasure and has brought me into contact with a large number of kind and helpful people. I should like to thank all those who have loaned me photographs and books and given me help and advice on my travels. A detailed list of photographic sources and acknowledgements is included at the end of the book but I should like to thank especially:

Alan Bentley, Bass Museum of Brewing, Burton-on-Trent; Martin Phillips, Keele University Library; Ray Poole, Leek Historical Society; George Short, Cheadle Historical Society; Pat Turner, Uttoxeter Heritage Centre; Basil Jeuda; Geoffrey Sowerby; Richard Farman; Rosalind Shipsides and Amanda Hansford, Shugborough Museum; Alan Taylor, Hanley Museum; Dudley Fowkes and the staff at the William Salt Library, Stafford; David Mills, Walsall Leather Centre and the staff at a variety of libraries all over the county.

Finally, thanks to my own family, Sue, Rupert and Tom for their patience whilst I was compiling the book and to my parents, Ray and Barbara Buxton, for providing a base and putting me up so often during my trips around the county.

David Buxton
July 1993

# Introduction

Staffordshire is a county with a variety of natural landscapes, from the rugged beauty of its moorland reaches in the north that merge with the Peaklands of Derbyshire, to the gentler charms of the valleys of the Dove and the Manifold, and from the great expanse of heath and woodland that is Cannock Chase, the hunting ground of kings, to the higher lands along the valley of the Trent where dairy cattle graze. Man has added his own contribution to the variety of scenery in some parts of Staffordshire and it is to the Industrial Revolution that we must look for the origins of some of these unnatural features of the landscape which are the inevitable associates of rapid growth in major manufacturing areas. Although, travelling in these parts of Staffordshire today one is much less aware of the bleaker aspects of this industrial legacy, a century ago one would have been in no doubt about why one of these areas became known, first popularly, and then officially, as the Black Country.

There are major coalfields in the north and south of the county which provided the fuel for this industrial growth but, initially, it was timber from the great forests that was used for smelting the iron found in this region. At the height of the Black Country's industrial activities the area was notorious for its smoke, factories and slag-heaps. It produced coal for the nation's factories and the south of the county contained some of the world's largest manufacturers of iron and specialist ironmongery. Each of the towns in the area had its speciality, indeed, some still do: buckles, bits and bridles at Walsall, chains at Cradley, locks and keys at Wolverhampton and tubes and axles at West Bromwich. At Walsall, leatherworking was also a major activity and sometimes the two were combined in leather-covered ironwork, such as leather buckles, for which Walsall was particularly famous.

An interesting story demonstrates how influential were these manufacturers: when, in the late eighteenth century, shoelaces

KEELE HALL

looked like becoming a fashionable replacement for shoe buckles, the Walsall buckle-makers feared for their future and in 1792 petitioned the Prince of Wales, later George IV, to ban these new-fangled devices from court and not to wear them himself. He agreed and for a while the fashion for laces in Britain was successfully suppressed and a specialized trade was preserved a little longer, by royal decree.

Although the Black Country's industry scarred the landscape with its spoil heaps and smoke, it also brought a prosperity to the area that was unprecedented. Great personal wealth was probably only enjoyed by a few, the owners of the great factories and mines, but the workers who created the wealth with their labours were certainly not made rich by their long hours of work and were often sadly exploited. Probably many of them considered themselves better off, though, than their counterparts in the country areas where there was great unemployment and hardship. The worst agricultural depression in history was devastating the countryside in the late 1880s and many farms were being forced out of business; a series of poor harvests in that decade had been to blame, finally making it impossible for many home farmers to compete with the cheap food imports that by this time flowed in from across the Atlantic. It was the resulting drift from country to town in the search for work and a better way of life that provided the workforce for the great industrial expansions of the nineteenth century. Some of the photographs and tales in this book show how poorly housed and fed were some of these workers.

Although the industrial wealth may have been unfairly shared, some of it was put to good public use. There is a legacy of fine, late Victorian building in many of the towns of the county. Museums, art galleries, libraries and grand municipal buildings abound in many of them. Wolverhampton and Walsall, particularly, retain some spectacular examples of late nineteenth century civic pride in their public buildings and parks. The citizens of these towns had the opportunity, at least, to enjoy some of the benefits of the wealth they had helped to create. The libraries and workers' institutes gave the opportunity for self-help and there were many examples of this; people who had received little or no chance of anything more than a rudimentary schooling would often spend years of their limited spare time in private study at these, often well-stocked, institutions, and with luck could hoist themselves a little higher up the ladder. While there were members of the privileged classes who thought this a proper provision for the poor and applauded such application of the Victorian work ethic, there would have been others who considered it a dangerous thing to educate the labouring classes who might then, in their turn, expect privileges above their station.

That other great area of industrial activity in the county, the Potteries, is perhaps the one best known to outsiders as Staffordshire's own industry. Although, at different times over the centuries, pottery has been made in most parts of Britain, it was in the eighteenth century that a group of small towns and villages in North Staffordshire began to diversify and produce, as well as the local slipware, a range of new pottery

FIRING THE POTTERS' OVENS

4

GLAZING PLATES

and fine porcelains and became the undisputed centre of the pottery industry. Its products were exported all over the world and the industry thrived. One man, in particular, was responsible for revolutionizing this industry, and that was Josiah Wedgewood, who arrived to partner Thomas Whieldon at his works in Fenton in 1752. About fifteen years later he set up his own great works at Etruria. As well as being a great craftsman and innovator he was also an astute businessman. He was largely responsible for persuading the Trent and Mersey Canal Company to route their all important waterway through the Potteries, an important factor in the development of the area. On Wedgewood's tomb in Stoke it is inscribed that he 'converted a rude and inconsiderable manufactory into an elegant art'.

The growth of the industry created a landscape that was peculiar to the area, with the characteristically-shaped, brick-built bottle-ovens rising up in nearly every street and pouring black smoke from their chimneys as they were fired. The photographic record of the late nineteenth-century period clearly shows how densely packed together were these kilns and how heavily polluted the atmosphere around them must have been. Fortunately, there is a very good photographic record of life in the towns of this period and some excellent scenes from the factories too.

Stoke today is still a major centre for pottery production but the only bottle-ovens to be seen are in the museum. All the modern kilns are electrically fired. Unlike the potteries, much of the industry that thrived a century ago in Staffordshire has no modern counterpart. Among those that were not able to compete with changing demands or cheaper competition was the textile industry. In the northern towns of Staffordshire, textile mills were usually the main employer but now the tape-mills at Tean and silk-mills at Cheadle and Leek are no more but at least, through the excellent accounts of that intrepid traveller and photographer, Mr Nithsdale, we can read about conditions in at least one of the mills at Leek, at the turn of the century (p 103). Another factory not far away from these mills, Thomas Bolton's at Oakamoor, enjoyed the distinction of having produced the copper cable that was laid under the Atlantic for the first telegraph link between Europe and America. When, soon after laying, this enormous cable failed, Thomas Bolton's factory promptly produced another one.

Over on the eastern border of the county, where the River Trent runs into Derbyshire, is an industry that has made this corner of Staffordshire world famous for at least one hundred and fifty years. Burton on Trent, by the second half of the nineteenth century, was the undisputed centre of the brewing industry. In 1887 Alfred Barnard conducted a survey of 'noted breweries of Great Britain and Ireland' and following a visit to Burton wrote a splendid account of the town's major activity. He observed:

> Since the twelfth century the trade of malting and brewing has been carried out in Burton, but it is only during the last fifty years that it has developed itself in such an extraordinary manner. As far back as AD 1295, the Abbots of Burton brewed conventional beer, and succeeding generations have but perfected what they began, until the brewing industry of Burton has reached a point which has no parallel in the world, and now contains as many as thirty-one breweries, giving employment to upwards of 8,000 persons. Driving along through the town, we were confronted on all sides by lofty buildings, in blocks of two or three ranges, as big as the Houses of Parliament, principally constructed of red brick, occasionally over-topped by huge water towers, all consecrated to the death and resurrection of John Barleycorn.

The enormous scale of beer production in Burton at this time is hard to comprehend. With so many breweries operating and with most of the working population employed in them, the industry totally dominated life in the town. Railway lines supplied each part of each brewery, criss-crossing the roads and streets of the town like a web and making a journey across Burton one of constant interruptions. Everywhere men would be seen rolling casks or unloading hops and barley sacks. The annual output of the largest of these breweries, Bass and Co., was one million barrels and so lucrative was the trade for its owners that the Bass family were amongst the richest in the land. The newspaper report of the wedding of Lord Bass's daughter, Nellie, in 1894 shows just how rich and influential the big brewers had become. The guest and present lists read like those of a royal wedding and even the people of Burton presented her with a diamond necklace. Fortunately, the Bass family were also renowned for their philanthropy. Sir Michael Bass, in particular, was responsible for a variety of public buidings and schemes in Burton and also in Derby, for whom he was the Member of Parliament.

Workers at the Bass breweries benefited from an annual outing, known as 'The Trip', which was provided at company expense. A fleet of trains took everyone to the seaside and the high level of precision with which these events were planned can be seen from the surviving 'Trip books' that were issued to the staff. So detailed are they that they read like a set of military battle plans. They included detailed instructions for the journey, urging good behaviour on the trains and noting the need to preserve 'the company's good image' whilst away. Although there were some helpful notes about what to look out for from the train windows there were also serious warnings about the hazards of dropping orange peel on the platform and putting your head out of the carriage window! I have used some extracts from one of these books in the main text that follows.

While there is a good photographic record of working life in many of these industries, a great deal of the surviving picture records of the late Victorian period often seems to be of celebrations and leisure events. This is a distortion of the course of true events because, like today, the camera tended to be used to record the unusual rather than the ordinary; the holidays and the parades rather than the routines of life. I have tried to even out this imbalance in the records by choosing photographs that show a more representative range of activities and scenes, both work and leisure, but trying to avoid giving the impression that life at the end of the nineteenth century was mainly spent celebrating Queen Victoria's Jubilees!

The extensive archive of photographs from this period is largely due to the prolific output of the High Street photographers who systematically recorded their town's streets and people, often for the production of postcards. While these pictures provide a valuable record of the period they are often, it has to be said, rather dull representations of streets, buildings and, of course, celebrations. It is refreshing sometimes, therefore, to come across the work of photographers that is not from this mould, people who chose to take, perhaps, a more candid scene in a market crowd or a well-posed group of subjects, that makes their work stand out from the rest. Examples of photographers in Staffordshire that stood out in this way included Simnett in Stafford, Richard Keene of Burton (and Derby) and Benjamin Stone from Birmingham, who took some stunning photographs in many of the Midland's towns and villages. Keene's photographs of the breweries at Burton are not only exceptionally sharp and clear but show his flair for choosing an unusual viewpoint (pp. 30, 106). Stone's studies of people, in particular, were outstanding; children receiving their traditional Bower Cakes at Lichfield (front endpapers) is a good example. There are many other examples of outstanding photography here too but we don't always know who the photographers were; there are some particularly good examples of informal scenes taken by different photographers at both Wolverhampton and Uttoxeter markets (pp. 61, 62, 103) and some of the series of record pictures taken in the potteries, from the Warrillow Collection are, by any standards, also exceptionally sensitive portraits (front cover, pp. 13, 17).

Alongside these visual images of late Victorian Staffordshire are a series of extracts from books, newspapers and other contemporary sources which, I hope, support and help to bring alive the pictures. I could not resist including amongst these a few extracts and a short story of the fictional accounts of life in the Potteries written by the man who put this region on the national map. Arnold Bennett's famous characters of 'The Five Towns' are vividly portrayed and drawn from his own childhood experience in the area. His decision to set the

stories within a fictional 'five towns' instead of the actual six towns of Stoke-on-Trent was explained by him in 1928 in a reply to the traders of Fenton who had asked why their town had been excluded from his popular books. He was quite blunt, one town had to be left out, he said, because he preferred the sound of 'five towns' to 'six towns'. The 'i' in 'six' is a closed vowel sound and is not so striking, he felt, as the open vowel sound of the 'i' in 'five'. He wanted a 'broad sounding' phrase for the district and chose Fenton as the one town to exclude because it was the smallest of the towns at the time. He renamed the towns but not so drastically that most are not still recognizable; thus Hanley became Hanbridge, Burslem became Bursley, Tunstall became Turnhill, Longton became Longshaw, but Stoke became Knype.

Now, having looked briefly at some of the historical background to the source of the photographs and text that make up this book, I hope you will go on to enjoy them in this new presentation, providing as they do, a glimpse of Staffordshire of around one hundred years ago.

# STAFFORDSHIRE

*of one hundred years ago*

BURTON ON TRENT

## THE BEER METROPOLIS

Starting from Derby at nine o'clock, we reached the Beer Metropolis in just eighteen minutes, and as we had an hour to spare before our appointment with Mr Clay (one of the Directors of the Company), we drove through the principal streets to see the locality, and map out our tour of the Breweries. Burton is a busy town, with a population of 40,000, and its long streets, which are everywhere intersected by level railway crossings, present a very animated scene.

Were it not for the vast breweries, which give life to the place, Burton would have ever remained an old fashioned, sleepy town.

Burton is pleasantly situated in a fertile vale on the western bank of the Trent, a beautiful river, which flows on the side of the town opposite to that occupied by the railway, past the picturesque grounds of the abbey, the recreation fields, and public gardens, to be referred to hereafter. Strangers from a distance imagine that the celebrated Burton beer is brewed from the Trent water; such, however, is not the case; it is only used by the brewers for cooling, washing, and other useful purposes. The brewing water comes from wells and bore-holes, which abound in the district, and have been sunk all over the town at an enormous expense.

Since the twelfth century the trade of malting and brewing has been carried on in Burton, but it is only during the last fifty years that it has developed itself in such an extraordinary manner.

As far back as AD 1295, the old Abbots of Burton brewed conventional beer, and succeeding generations have but perfected what they began, until the brewing industry of Burton has reached a point which has no parallel in the world, and now contains as many as thirty-one breweries, giving employment to upwards of 8,000 persons. Driving along through the town, we were confronted on all sides by lofty buildings, in blocks of two or three ranges, as big as the Houses of Parliament, principally constructed of red brick, occasionally over-topped by huge water towers, all consecrated to the death and resurrection of John Barleycorn.

Every now and then, we got a peep through wide gateways down the long yards of the breweries, where whole armies of men were diligently employed in making and washing casks,

SOUP DISTRIBUTION, BURTON ON TRENT

rolling barrels, loading or unloading casks and raw materials into railway trucks, waggons and floaters.

The business of Messrs Bass & Co. was founded by William Bass, in the year 1777. He was born in the year 1720, and was the great grandfather of the present chief partner, Lord Burton, and the house in which he dwelt, and wherein his son and grandson were born, still flanks the gateway of the old brewery. When first started, Bass's brewery, in High Street, turned out about 6,000 barrels per annum; but, before the beginning of the present century, the business had so increased that the size of the brewery was doubled. In 1853, a second brewery was erected and, exactly ten years later, a third. The old brewery, which from time to time had been enlarged, was rebuilt in the years 1884 and 1885 and, although still called the old brewery, it is, in reality, the newest of the group, and contains many new appliances and modern machinery inventions known to the art of brewing. Messrs Bass & Co.'s three establishments now cover 145 acres of ground, and, together, form the largest ale and bitter brewery in the world.

Like the great firms of Guinness, the brewers, and Roe & Co., the distillers of Dublin, who each restored a cathedral at an immense cost, the Burton brewers have not been behind-hand in liberality.

The late Michael Thomas Bass built and endowed one of the finest churches in the Midland Counties with a vicarage, a chapel of ease, and Sunday-school. He also built an institute at Burton-on-Trent, a public library, baths and recreation ground at Derby, and a handsome church and institute at Rangemore, the whole costing nearly £200,000. In 1884, Mr M.T. Bass died, deeply lamented both in his native town and Derby (which he had represented in Parliament for thirty-three years), and throughout the country. He was a man of great industry, integrity and business capacity, and was very proud of the great business he had built up. His benefactions were numerous, not only in his native town but throughout the district, and he laboured unceasingly for the good of his fellow-men both in his public and private life. A few years previous to his death, the business was turned into a private Limited Company, of which his eldest son, now Lord Burton, is Chairman.

*Alfred Barnard*

## PENNY READINGS

As the immediate consequence of the great interest taken in the public readings from *The Times* war correspondence at the Market Terrace, Hanley, penny readings were initiated, the Potteries having the distinction of being the first place where these popular entertainments were held. The promoter was Mr S. Taylor, formerly identified with the *Sentinel*, as part proprietor.

TUNSTALL

About the time that the paper duty was done away with, the readings became popular. The merchants, shopkeepers, &c., and others, whose education was above that of the average of the town in those days, would entertain large audiences by these means. The evenings were not spent solely in literary readings, but these were occasionally interspersed with songs by amateurs, and instrumental music by amateurs and professional men. Well-known men would occasionally come down, such as Mr Mark Lemon, Charles Dickens, and the Grossmith's pere et fils. As the native singers were talented they were largely relied upon, quite a number of female singers making their appearance about this period. Tastes, like fashions, change, and gradually the entertainments came to an end. One may say they had a good run for eight or ten years.

*William Scarratt*

## HANLEY AND THE PREACHER

I was instructed to go to Hanley, and reached the town on the 31st of December, 1881, accompanied by my wife and one child. The baby was just a year old. It was a Saturday when I arrived. The General had said to me some days before, 'Where do you want to go to next?' I answered, 'Send me to the nearest place to the bottomless pit.' When I got to Stoke station, and began to make my way on the loop-line to Hanley, the pit fires came in sight, and I could smell the sulphur of the iron foundries, and see the smoke from the potteries; I began to wonder if I had not got to the actual place whither I had asked to be sent. At Hanley station we engaged a cab, got our trunks on it, and went off in search of lodgings. For two hours we drove over the town, knocking at many doors. But when we said that we were a contingent of the Salvation Army, the portals were shut against us. At last a poor old Welsh body took compassion on us and took us in.

I went at once to see the battlefield, namely, the building in which the services were to be held. Three young men had been sent to the town to commence operations two or three weeks before our arrival, but they had utterly failed to make any impression on the people. The meetings were held in the old Batty Circus, a cold, draughty, tumbledown sort of place, the most uncomfortable meeting-house in which I had ever worked. The ring of the circus had been left just as it was

FOUNTAIN SQUARE, HANLEY

when the circus people cleared out, and any one who ventured therein was soon up to the knees in sawdust and dirt. There were no seats in this portion of the circus. On this Saturday evening I found two young lieutenants standing inside the ring, making it a sort of pulpit. Sprinkled over the seats of the building, rising tier upon tier, were from twenty to thirty people, looking for all the world like jam-pots on a shelf, and singing as I entered, 'I need Thee, oh, I need Thee.' Believe me, I stood and laughed. I thought it was true enough that they needed somebody. After a brief talk with the people I asked them to meet me in the Market Place at ten o'clock next morning.

The two young lieutenants, my wife and myself, duly took our stand in the Market Place on Sunday morning. Not a soul came out to support us. I played a little concertina which had been given to me on leaving Devonport by my friends there, many of whom were converts. We sang some hymns, and people living above the shops in the Market Place, thinking we were labourers out of work, threw us pennies. I had no uniform on, in fact, I got out of wearing the uniform when I could, and, indeed, never in my life did I wear a red jersey. I used to dress somewhat, although not markedly, in gipsy fashion. Nobody stopped to listen to us. It was rather wet, and

the people who passed by on their way to church put their umbrellas in front of their faces so that we should not see them. But we went on as though we had been addressing a crowd. In the afternoon, the four of us were in the open-air again. At night, about eighty people attended our services in the circus. The building seated 2,500 people, but these eighty people huddling themselves close together, to keep warm I suppose (for the building was very cold), sat in the midst of the most appalling and depressing desolation. It was a very dismal beginning, without hope, without cheer, without anything that gave promise of success.

But I was resolved to do what I could in this difficult situation. On Monday morning we went to the building to see if we could do something to stop the draughts and get the windows mended. We found a hammer, some nails, and some pieces of timber in the empty stable of the circus, and we worked with these instruments all day, doing our best to make the place habitable. My wife assisted by holding a candle when we had to creep into dark corners in the course of our labours. I sometimes nowadays marvel at the great mechanical skill which we discovered among ourselves. It is wonderful what a man can do, even a man who knows himself to be unskilled, when he is put to it. For two weeks we went on

LICHFIELD

hammering and plastering, and then I secured the help of my brother-in-law, Mr Evens, a joiner by trade. He spent a few days with us, and in that time we made some seats for the ring. We got hold of some old chairs, knocked the backs off and planked them together.

In the meantime we continued our services in the Market Place and our audience grew quickly to large proportions. The people listened attentively, and joined heartily in the singing. But we had never more than a hundred people in the circus. After a month's hard labour I asked the General for help – something in the way of a special attraction. I felt we were not making progress quickly enough. The first month's collections just managed to pay the gas bill. There was no money for the poor evangelists, and no money for the rent. We did not apply for pecuniary assistance, because every station was supposed to be self-supporting, and we had made up our minds that Hanley would pay its way too. The General gave us the services of the 'Fry family', a father and three sons, splendid musicians, for a few days. They could sing beautifully and play almost any instrument. It occurred to me that if I could get somebody of local reputation to preside at their first meeting we should have a good congregation. I was advised to call on the Mayor of Burslem, who that year was Alderman Boulton, and ask him to preside. It so happened that the Revd John Gould, who was then Wesleyan minister at Hull, had just been with the Mayor, and had told him about my work in that great city. On the strength of Mr Gould's report, Alderman Boulton promised to preside at the first of the Fry meetings.

I at once got out a huge poster, announcing that a great

HANLEY

ROCK HOUSES, KINVER

public meeting in connection with the Salvation Army was to be held in the Batty Circus, that the Mayor of Burslem would preside, that various speakers would address the gathering, and that the singing would be led by the Fry family. The Alderman was kind enough to invite a good many of his friends, substantial business men, to accompany him to the meeting, so that the platform was filled, and there was a crowded attendance. The Alderman plainly discerned what had been our purpose in organising this meeting, and his speech was indeed a master-stroke. He told the people tersely, though fully, all about my work at Hull, and then he said, 'We have not heard Gipsy Smith, and we all want to hear him. I am not going to take up your time. The Gipsy will address the meeting.' I was ready and willing, proud indeed to face such a magnificent audience. My sermon was very short, for I desired to get the people back again, and so I sent them away hungry. I never wanted a congregation after that meeting. As long as we occupied this old circus it was crowded at every service. The Mayor had placed the local hall-mark on our work, and we at once entered into the good-will of the whole town.

The work in Hanley, once well begun, went on increasing in success and fruitfulness. The revival which had its centre in our meeting-place spread over the whole of North Staffordshire. There was no Nonconformist Church within ten or twenty miles of Hanley that did not feel the throb of it. At the end of every week hundreds and thousands of persons poured into Hanley, the metropolis of the Potteries, to attend our meetings. From 6.30 p.m. on Saturday to 9.30 p.m. on Sunday we had nine services, indoors and out of doors. I conducted them all. We sold ten thousand copies of *The War Cry* every week. No other station in the Salvation Army has ever managed to do this, as far as I know. I cannot go into any congregation in the Potteries to-day without seeing people who were converted under my ministry in that great revival. In America and in Australia too I have met converts of those days. I preached every Sunday to crowds of from seven thousand to eight thousand people, and every night in the week we had the place crowded for an evangelistic service.

*Gipsy Smith*

VELOCIPEDES

## My First Bicycle Ride

I was young, I was also ambitious, accordingly, one fine Wednesday morning, some years ago, I was sitting in the Writing Room, diligently taking down 'History Notes', when, all of a sudden, a brilliant idea (at least so it seemed to me at that time), crossed my mind – I would go for a bicycle ride that afternoon, as it was a holiday; that was to say, if I could get anyone else to accompany me; for I was at that time possessed of a bicycle, a 46-inch, which I could just reach, and which, though covered with rust all over, nevertheless, served as a means of locomotion. Now I had to take great care in choosing a companion for my proposed expedition, for it was necessary that that companion should be able to ride fairly well, and to mount and dismount his machine without assistance, as at that time I was able to achieve neither of these exploits. And so, when the Master's back was turned for a time, I crept under two or three desks to a fellow who was about the same size as myself, and asked him if he would join me; he said he should be delighted only he had at that time no bicycle, having lent his own to a friend: but, not to be discouraged, I told him I thought that I could borrow one, and by creeping under two or three more desks, I reached a

boy who possessed a machine. Upon my asking him for the loan of it, he said he should be delighted to lend it to me for that afternoon, as he was not going to use it himself. Thereupon I returned under the desks, and informed my friend that I had procured a bicycle; but, as he was not much more proficient than myself in the art of riding, it was necessary that we should find yet a third, more experienced than either of us.

At last after some consultation, by means of notes passed from one to the other, we settled on one whom we believed to be an experienced rider, and who might be persuaded to accompany us. At twelve o'clock when the bell rang, we looked out anxiously for him, and when, after we had hunted him out, he said he would accompany us, our delight was unbounded. After a good deal of conversation we fixed on the route that we should pursue, selecting, chiefly by the advice of our Guide, the Stafford Road, as being best suited to such amateurs as ourselves.

We then separated, my friend and myself going anxiously home to dinner, the third, our Guide and Guardian, walking off in a leisurely manner and evincing none of the emotion that we betrayed.

Arriving home, having run nearly all the way from School,

LOWER GREEN, TETTENHALL

THE FIRST BICYCLE

I scrambled through my dinner in a state of great excitement, and the instant that I had finished – and as anyone may guess I had not eaten much, nor taken a very long time over it – I rushed off to look at my machine. There it stood, covered with rust from top to bottom, nevertheless, I flattered myself that 'looks went for nothing', and so, having expended all the oil I could find in lubricating the bearings, pedals, head, etc., I started off, wheeling my machine through the town, as I could not trust myself to riding in the streets, and even if I had dared to do this, the mounting the machine would have proved an insurmountable obstacle. At length I arrived at my friend's residence, and found him in a state of excitement equal to, or, if possible, greater than that in which I myself was; together we wended our way to borrow the machine for him, which, having been successfully accomplished, we proceeded to look up our Guide, still wheeling the bicycles, as my friend, like myself, had not arrived at such a stage of proficiency in bicycling, as to be able to mount his machine, though he informed me with some pride that he *could get off*. He afterwards proved that he was justified in making this assertion.

We found our Guide ready to start, and accordingly, having got clear of the centre of the town, we mounted – or rather he put us on, which, I remember, was accomplished by leaning his own machine against the nearest wall or lamp-post, and after helping us on in turn, himself mounting and catching us up again – and made for Four Ashes.

We went down the Waterloo Road, and all seemed to be getting on swimmingly, when, just opposite the Molineux Grounds, from some unaccountable reason, my back wheel gave a jump which caused me to reach the ground, via the

DARLINGTON STREET, WOLVERHAMPTON

handles. Nothing dismayed, I got put on again and we made a fresh start, and proceeded to the Stafford Road Works without mishap, and then ahead of me I saw the hill up to Oxley; it looked steep, much steeper than it had ever seemed before when I had been walking or driving, but nevertheless, I determined to try to ride up it, so I put on a spurt but narrowly escaped a second fall by riding over a stone, which I had seen a long way off, and which had exercised a kind of magic influence over my big wheel. The spurt soon came to an end, and I began to wobble, and at last came to a dead stop, so that my machine gently sidled over and deposited me in the road; I got up and picked the machine up also, and noticed that my friend had been similarly deposited in the road, a little farther down the hill. Our Guide had by this time reached the top, and was waiting for us, so we wheeled our machines up to him, and getting put on again, 'rattled' merrily down the other side. We now seemed to be gaining by experience, and rode on without accident to the Ford Houses. Here my friend narrowly escaped running over a horse and cart, his right-hand pedal just missing one of the wheels, he pretended that he had done so on purpose to give us a fright, but I fancy he succeeded in giving himself one. We proceeded onwards, walking up the Coven bridges, as our failure at Oxley was still fresh in our memory, and at length arrived at Four Ashes in an hour-and-a-half from our starting. Here we refreshed the 'inner man', or rather the 'inner boy', and our spirits were so raised by ginger beer that we resolved that we would go to Brewood and to Wolverhampton that way, instead of returning by the same road that we had come.

WIGHTWICK

ALTON

So we started for Brewood, thinking what heroes we should be when we arrived at home after such a long ride. My own spirits were so high that I began to ride on the foot-path, defying all policemen and such like. I got on splendidly for a time, keeping about thirty yards in advance of my two companions, when suddenly I thought that I descried a figure in a blue uniform on ahead, the figure looked uncommonly like a 'bobby', so I thought I had better get out into the middle of the road. This was rather difficult as the footpath was raised about six inches above the level of the road, and in looking out for a convenient place to get off I ran into the hedge. I fell one way, my machine the other, the latter coming down with a loud thump. I picked myself up and went to examine the bicycle. It seemed to be none the worse with the exception of the left pedal having become loose; this I thought could be easily remedied with the aid of a spanner, but I had not brought mine, and on enquiring of my friend I found there was not one in the bag attached to his machine, and our Guide's would not fit the nut. I tightened it as well as I could with my fingers, and, having been put on again, rode on, my ardour having been rather damped by my fall. We soon caught up the 'individual in blue', who proved to be no policeman as I had imagined, but only a rustic, who gave us a cheer as we passed, which so excited us that my friend and I all but ran into each other.

We reached Brewood in about an hour-and-an-half from Four Ashes, having lost our way, and gone about two miles further than was necessary; there had only been one mishap since we had seen the countryman – my friend having had a spill over the handles, and bent the crank of his machine a little – though I had had to be helped off several times in order to tighten my pedal, which kept coming loose. At Brewood I bought half a pound of biscuits, having been given sixpence before I started, which my friend and myself proceeded to eat, our Guide refusing to eat more than one, my friend had also purchased some chocolate, which made us very thirsty. We wheeled our machines till we were clear of the town, and then were put on once more by our good-natured Guide. My friend and I now began to feel the effects of riding so far, and our spirits were fast evaporating, though the biscuits and chocolate at Brewood had raised them a little. At last we reached Coven, where a school-fellow resided, and he, thoughtful youth, upon seeing us, began to pelt us with shot from his catapult, whereupon I tumbled off my steed through fear of getting hit. At length we reached the canal bridge, and upon our telling the Guide there was 'no hurry', he took the hint and helped us off, and we all rested on the bridge for about ten minutes. Upon re-mounting we rode all the way to the bottom of the Oxley Hill without accident of any kind, but failed to ride up, and took good care that we were not put

18

BURTON ON TRENT MARKET

on again till we were past the top. The hill at the Stafford Road Works proved a formidable obstacle, but by dint of much perseverance we overcame it, and rode on up the Waterloo Road. I felt awfully tired, though I did not say so, but I proved that I was when I had my last fall at very nearly the same spot as my first, viz: opposite the Molineux Grounds, in endeavouring to ride up the slight hill there. My friend, with much exertion and wobbling, managed to ride up it, but ran over a stone at the top and fell off. He refused the offer of our guide to be put on again, and I did the same, so we wheeled our machines to the top of the Waterloo Road, where, after having been informed by our guide that we had ridden 26 miles (I am afraid he exaggerated a little), we separated, my friend taking his machine back to its owner, and I myself making the best of my way home.

I was very glad when I reached my paternal mansion, and made up for my bad dinner by a very good tea, and after it I did little or no work, but read an exciting tale which was then appearing in the *Boys' Own Paper*.

Such, reader, was my first Bicycle Ride. Since then I have been on many longer ones, but none that I can recall to mind so well.

In conclusion, I would advise any who are ambitious to go for a long ride, if they are not experienced cyclists, to choose a companion who can ride well, and who would be as good-

natured as ours was. Though a little troublesome at first, I am sure, there is no amusement more healthy or more pleasurable than 'Cycling'.

*The Walfrunian (Wolverhampton School magazine),* 1885

## ON THE BANK

'I suppose we had better start at the start,' he said, leading the way to the slip-house. He did not need to be told that Anna was perfectly ignorant of the craft of pottery, and that every detail of it, so stale to him, would acquire freshness under her naïve and inquiring gaze.

In the slip-house begins the long manipulation which transforms raw porous friable clay into the moulded, decorated, and glazed vessel. The large whitewashed place was occupied by ungainly machines and receptacles through which the four sorts of clay used in the common 'body' – ball clay, China clay, flint clay, and stone clay – were compelled to pass before they became a white putty-like mixture meet for shaping by human hands. The blunger crushed the clay, the sifter extracted the iron from it by means of a magnet, the press expelled the water, and the pug-mill expelled the air. From the last reluctant mouth slowly emerged a solid stream

BOTTLE OVENS, LONGTON

MAKING DOLLS' HEADS, LONGTON

nearly a foot in diameter, like a huge white snake. Already the clay had acquired the uniformity characteristic of a manufactured product.

Anna moved to touch the bolts of the enormous twenty-four-chambered press.

'Don't stand there,' said Mynors. 'The pressure is tremendous, and if the thing were to burst –'

She fled hastily. 'But isn't it dangerous for the workmen?' she asked.

Eli Machin, the engineman, the oldest employee on the works, a moneyed man, and the pattern of reliability, allowed a vague smile to flit across his face at this remark. He had ascended from the engine-house below in order to exhibit the tricks of the various machines, and that done he disappeared. Anna was awed by the sensation of being surrounded by terrific forces always straining for release and held in check by the power of a single wall.

'Come and see a plate made: that is one of the simplest things, and the batting-machine is worth looking at,' said Mynors, and they went into the nearest shop, a hot interior in the shape of four corridors round a solid square middle. Here men and women were working side by side, the women

subordinate to the men. All were preoccupied, wrapped up in their respective operations, and there was the sound of irregular whirring movements from every part of the big room. The air was laden with whitish dust, and clay was omnipresent – on the floor, the walls, the benches, the windows, on clothes, hands, and faces. It was in this shop, where both hollow-ware pressers and flat pressers were busy as only craftsmen on piecework can be busy, that more than anywhere else clay was to be seen 'in the hand of the potter'. Near the door a stout man with a good-humoured face flung some clay on to a revolving disc, and even as Anna passed a jar sprang into existence. One instant the clay was an amorphous mass, the next it was a vessel particularly circular, of a prescribed width and a prescribed depth; the flat and apparently clumsy fingers of the craftsman had seemed to lose themselves in the clay for a fraction of time, and the miracle was accomplished. The man threw these vessels with the rapidity of a Roman candle throwing off coloured stars, and one woman was kept busy in supplying him with material and relieving his bench of the finished articles. Mynors drew Anna along to the batting-machines for plate makers, at that period rather a novelty and the latest invention of the dead genius

LONGTON

PREPARING CLAY

whose brain has reconstituted a whole industry on new lines. Confronted with a piece of clay, the batting-machine descended upon it with a ferocity of a wild animal, worried it, stretched it, smoothed it into the width and thickness of a plate, and then desisted of itself and waited inactive for the flat presser to remove its victim to his more exact shaping machine. Several men were producing plates, but their rapid labours seemed less astonishing than the preliminary feat of the batting-machine. All the ware as it was moulded disappeared into the vast cupboards occupying the centre of the shop, where Mynors showed Anna innumerable rows of shelves full of pots in process of steam-drying. Neither time nor space nor material was wasted in this ant-heap of industry. In order to move to and fro, the women were compelled to insinuate themselves past the stationary bodies of the men. Anna marvelled at the careless accuracy with which they fed the batting-machines with lumps precisely calculated to form a plate of a given diameter. Everyone exerted himself as though the salvation of the world hung on the production of so much stuff by a certain hour; dust, heat, and the presence of a stranger were alike unheeded in the mad creative passion.

'Now,' said Mynors the cicerone, opening another door which gave into the yard, 'when all that stuff is dried and fettled – smoothed, you know – it goes into the biscuit oven: that's the first firing. There's the biscuit oven, but we can't inspect it because it's just being drawn.'

He pointed to the oven nearby, in whose dark interior the forms of men, naked to the waist, could dimly be seen struggling with the weight of saggars full of ware. It seemed like some release of martyrs, this unpacking of the immense oven, which, after being flooded with a sea of flame for fifty-four hours, had cooled for two days, and was yet hotter than

CASTING CUPS FROM LIQUID CLAY

the Equator. The inertness and pallor of the saggars seemed to be the physical result of their fiery trial, and one wondered that they should have survived the trial. Mynors went into the place adjoining the oven, and brought back a plate out of an open saggar; it was still quite warm. It had the matt surface of a biscuit, and adhered slightly to the fingers: it was now a 'crook'; it had exchanged malleability for brittleness, and nothing mortal could undo what the fire had done. Mynors took the plate with him to the biscuit-warehouse, a long room where one was forced to keep to narrow alleys amid parterres of pots. A solitary biscuit-warehouseman was examining the ware in order to determine the remuneration of the pressers.

They climbed a flight of steps to the printing-shop, where, by means of copper-plates, printing-presses, mineral colours, and transfer-papers, most of the decoration was done. The room was filled by a little crowd of people – oldish men, women, and girls, divided into printers, cutters, transferrers, and apprentices. Each interminably repeated some trifling process, and every article passed through a succession of hands until at length it was washed in a tank and rose dripping therefrom with its ornament of flowers and scrolls fully revealed. The room smelt of oil and flannel and humanity; the atmosphere was more languid, more like that of a family party, than in the pressers' shop: the old women looked stern and shrewish, the pretty young women pert and defiant, the younger girls meek. The few men seemed out of place. By what trick had they crept into the very centre of that mass of femininity? It seemed wrong, scandalous that they should

STACKING SAGGARS IN A BOTTLE OVEN

23

DECORATING CHINA, LONGTON

remain. Contiguous with the printing-shop was the painting-shop, in which the labours of the former were taken to a finish by the brush of the paintress, who filled in outlines with flat colour, and thus converted mechanical printing into handiwork. The paintresses form the *noblesse* of the banks. Their task is a light one, demanding deftness first of all; they have delicate fingers, and enjoy a general reputation for beauty: the wages they earn may be estimated from their finery on Sundays. They come to business in cloth jackets, carry dinner in little satchels; in the shop they wear white aprons, and look startlingly neat and tidy. Across the benches over which they bend their coquettish heads gossip flies and returns like a shuttle; they are the source of a thousand intrigues, and one or other of them is continually getting married or omitting to get married. On the bank they constitute 'the sex'. An infinitesimal proportion of them, from among the branch known as ground-layers, die of lead-poisoning – a fact which adds pathos to their frivolous charm. In a subsidiary room off the painting-shop a single girl was seated at a revolving table actuated by a treadle. She was doing the 'band-and-line' on the rims of saucers. Mynors and Anna watched her as with her left hand she flicked saucer after saucer into the exact centre of the table, moved the treadle, and, holding a brush firmly against the rim of the piece,

produced with infallible exactitude the band and the line. She was a brunette, about twenty-eight: she had a calm, vacuously contemplative face; but God alone knew whether she thought. Her work represented the summit of monotony; the regularity of it hypnotized the observer, and Mynors himself was impressed by this stupendous phenomenon of absolute sameness, involuntarily assuming towards it the attitude of a showman.

'She earns as much as eighteen shillings a week sometimes,' he whispered.

'May I try?' Anna timidly asked of a sudden, curious to experience what the trick was like.

'Certainly,' said Mynors, in eager assent. 'Priscilla, let this lady have your seat a moment, please.'

The girl got up, smiling politely. Anna took her place.

'Here, try on this,' said Mynors, putting on the table the plate which he still carried.

'Take a full brush,' the paintress suggested, not attempting to hide her amusement at Anna's unaccustomed efforts. 'Now push the treadle. There! It isn't in the middle yet. Now!'

Anna produced a most creditable band, and a trembling but passable line, and rose flushed with the small triumph.

'You have the gift,' said Mynors; and the paintress respectfully applauded.

POTTER'S WHEEL, LONGTON

'I felt I could do it,' Anna responded. 'My mother's mother was a paintress, and it must be in the blood.'

Mynors smiled indulgently. They descended again to the ground floor, and following the course of manufacture came to the 'hardening-on' kiln, a minor oven where for twelve hours the oil is burnt out of the colour in decorated ware. A huge, jolly man in shirt and trousers, with an enormous apron, was in the act of drawing the kiln, assisted by two thin boys. He nodded a greeting to Mynors and exclaimed, 'Warm!' The kiln was nearly emptied. As Anna stopped at the door, the man addressed her.

'Step inside, miss, and try it.'

'No, thanks!' she laughed.

'Come now,' he insisted, as if despising this hesitation. 'An ounce of experience –' The two boys grinned and wiped their foreheads with their bare skeleton-like arms. Anna, challenged by the man's look, walked quickly into the kiln. A blasting heat seemed to assault her on every side, driving her back; it was incredible that any human being could support such a temperature.

'There!' said the jovial man, apparently summing her up with his bright, quizzical eyes. 'You know summat as you didn't know afore, miss. Come along, lads,' he added with brisk heartiness to the boys, and the drawing of the kiln proceeded.

Next came the dipping-house, where a middle-aged woman, enveloped in a protective garment from head to foot, was dipping jugs into a vat of lead-glaze, a boy assisting her. The woman's hands were covered with the grey, slimy glaze. She alone of all the employees appeared to be cool.

'That is the last stage but one,' said Mynors. 'There is only

DECORATING CHINA

CHINA WAREHOUSE

the glost-iring,' and they passed out into the yard once more. One of the glost-ovens was empty; they entered it and peered into the lofty inner chamber, which seemed like the cold crater of an exhausted volcano, or like a vault, or like the ruined seat of some forgotten activity. The other oven was firing, and Anna could only look at its exterior, catching glimpses of the red glow at its twelve mouths, and guess at the Tophet, within, where the lead was being fused into glass.

'Now for the glost-warehouse, and you will have seen all,' said Mynors, 'except the mould-shop, and that doesn't matter.'

The warehouse was the largest place on the works, a room sixty feet long and twenty broad, low, whitewashed, bare, and clean. Piles of ware occupied the whole of the walls and of the immense floor-space, but there was no trace here of the soilure and untidiness incident to manufacture; all processes were at an end, clay had vanished into crock: and the calmness and the whiteness atoned for the disorder, noise, and squalor which had preceded. Here was a sample of the total and final achievement towards which the thousands of small, disjointed efforts that Anna had witnessed, were directed. And it seemed a miraculous, almost impossible, result; so definite, precise, and regular after a series of acts apparently variable, inexact, and casual; so inhuman after all that intensely inhuman labour; so

vast in comparison with the minuteness of the separate endeavours.

*Arnold Bennett*

## DRINK AND THE DEATH RATE

The British Medical Association appointed a committee to make inquiries, in order to ascertain the average age of the different categories of drinkers, that is to say, those who refrain completely from alcoholic drink, those who indulge more or less in moderation, and those who drink to excess. This committee has handed in its report. Its conclusions are drawn from 4,234 deaths, which are divided into five categories of individuals, with the average age attained by each:

1. Total abstainers ....................................  51 years 22 days
2. Habitually temperate drinkers ..............  63  ”  13  ”
3. Careless drinkers .................................  59  ”  67  ”
4. Free drinkers ......................................  57  ”  59  ”
5. Decidedly intemperate drinkers ..........  53  ”  3  ”

These figures show, singularly enough, that those who reach the shortest age are those who drink no alcohol whatever;

after them come the drunkards, who only exceed them by a trifle. The greatest average age is reached by those who drink moderately.

*Daily Telegraph October 30, 1889*

## MADE IN WALSALL

The making of bits, stirrups, and spurs is one of the most ancient and important industries of Walsall. There are nearly 1,000 operatives employed in various branches of their manufacture, and these are carried on by about 50 different employers. Walsall supplies the greater proportion of bits for the consumption of the world, while the manufacture of stirrups and spurs is almost exclusively confined to Walsall. It is almost incredible that tons of those goods are produced weekly in Walsall. They are made of various materials, such as hand-forged and malleable iron, steel, nickel, and also of many combinations of metals which are patented for these special purposes. Some are plated with silver and some with nickel, and much skill and taste is expended upon their production. All kinds and qualities are produced in the town, from the elaborately chased and ornamented to the strong and cheap kinds which are required for the foreign and Colonial markets. Much ingenuity has been expended upon making stirrups which will ensure safety to the rider, and nearly every

manufacturer has obtained patents, which has tended to improve and increase the trade. It is said that the greater number of bits, spurs, and stirrups which obtain such fancy prices by being stamped by the merchant: 'London made' have had their origin in the workshops and manufactories of Walsall.

Brush making is carried on extensively in Walsall, and finds employment for several hundred hands of both sexes. The application of machinery during recent years has almost revolutionised the trade, which until a few years ago was one of the ancient handicrafts. A brush has to undergo many processes before it is turned out as a finished article, and nearly every country in the world has to be requisitioned to find suitable materials for its manufacture. Bristles are obtained from Siberia, Russia, India, and Poland; fibres from Mexico, Ceylon, and South Africa; weeds from Italy and South America; horse-hair from America, Australia, and China. For the backs and handles of brushes a large variety of material is also used, such as ivory, tortoiseshell, bone, woods of home and foreign growth, such as rosewood, satinwood, mahogany, beech, sycamore, and chestnut. The variety of brushes made is enormous, as they are used for all purposes, from painting a house to cleaning machinery, and polishing metal. It is not unusual for some firms to make 5,000 different kinds. During the late South African war it is computed that 20,000 brushes per week were dispatched from Walsall for the use of the troops.

The manufacture of buckles is one of the oldest industries

CHEADLE

of the town of which there is any record. During the last century the industry has grown enormously, largely owing to the enterprise and push of its manufacturers, and to-day 2,000 or 3,000 hands are employed in making every conceivable kind of buckle, from chased gold and silver buckles for State harness, down to the humble tinned and japanned buckles sold at as low as $6\frac{1}{2}$d. to $7\frac{1}{2}$d. per gross. Leather-covered buckles, too, originated in Walsall, and are still made in large quantities. Machinery is used very largely; some metal buckles are made entirely automatically, the human hand only being required to feed the machine. The markets for buckles made in Walsall may be correctly described as the whole world.

The making of chains, cart hames, and cart gears comprises a very large branch allied to the saddlery trade of Walsall. It consists of certain classes of iron goods used for agricultural purposes and for heavy draught harness. The production of these goods began almost at the same time that Walsall started as a manufacturing town of saddlery. Chain making is one of the oldest trades, which for centuries has always been carried on in the old-fashioned way by hand forging; but within recent years electricity has been requisitioned, and we are glad to say that Walsall has been the first to avail herself of this method of manufacture to any extent in England. Chains in their old state, when they were first introduced for the drawing of ploughs and agricultural work, were of a heavy description, but they finally evolved into lighter work, such as curbs, dog chains, manger chains, and all classes for saddlery and stable uses.

Whips and thongs of upwards of 1,000 varieties are made in

CHURCH HILL, WALSALL

29

SHERIFF'S RIDE AROUND THE LICHFIELD BOUNDARIES

Walsall from stocks of thread and cane, gut and whalebone, holly and thorn, and also by patent process from steel and cane, covered with gut or thread, for which there is an increasing demand. They are manufactured for all markets, both at home and abroad.

Although Walsall has been the home of gents' pigskin purses for some forty years, it is only during the last decade that any great advance has been made. Now a very large range of Morocco, seal, Russia, crocodile, lizard, and most other fancy leathers are utilised in the manufacture of various styles of purses, dollar bill, and letter cases, etc. While this portion of the trade has developed into a large and increasing industry, it only forms one of many branches, which include the manufacture of watch guards, wristlets, garters, jewel cases, blotters, collar boxes, brush cases, and a host of other side-lines.

Harness and saddlery, although not the original trade of the town, is now the staple trade, and the one for which Walsall is justly famed throughout the world. The number of people engaged in the various branches is at least 3,500, and if we include the women stitchers, whose services are requisitioned in times of great stress, such as the South African war, the number would be not less than 5,000. The term 'harness and saddlery' embraces a wide variety, ranging from the delicately embroidered Somerset saddle for the long journeys of South America, to the severely plain, workmanlike English hunter; from the tiny race saddle, weighing sometimes not more than

a pound, to the large, cumbrous patterns beloved of the South African farmer; from the extremely light harness for American sulkies and for show purposes, to the heaviest styles for cart, plough, and dray; and from the highly-finished London carriage harness, to the rough, untrimmed and unbeautiful West Indian mule pattern. All are in the day's work, and alike welcomed by the manufacturer, whose interests are not confined to one market, but who 'surveys mankind from China to Peru' in his search for business, and whose desire is not to thrust his own ideas on the buyers of his goods, but to give them the article which their experience teaches is the best.

*Walsall: Past and Present, 1905*

## FLASH PRACTICE

Flash is perched high on a slope immediately south of Axe Edge, a few hundred yards off the high-way. It has some pretension to fame in possessing the highest church in England. Flash also has a history unique in the kingdom, but not yet of sufficient antiquity to give it the niche and homage it deserves. Here a century ago or more, it is averred, there settled a Nomadic tribe, who were skilled in every swindling trick and artifice then in vogue at fair and market. To them is assigned the doubtful honour of the inventions of Flash notes

OX ROAST, STAPENHILL

and spurious coin; but as coin and notes and dishonesty have been human attributes from time immemorial, I would not readily condemn the Gipsies on that count. In any circumstances, however, the people of Flash settled their scores in illegitimate cash, and either the cash, or this particular neighbourhood, derived the pseudonym thereby. And these same people of Flash eluded the tardy justice of those days through the facilities afforded them by their highland homes.

We drove around the sharp bend at Flash Bar, and a little further along, at the next turn, left the high-road, for Knotbury. And as we journeyed into the moorland fastnesses, we saw farmsteads, some high upon almost inaccessible hill sides, some deep down in wild ravines, which stamped the history of Flash with the hall-mark of possibility.

We left our carriage in a bye-path and walked down a steep, stony cart-track to Three Shire Heads, where the counties of Derby, Stafford and Chester are separated only by the confluence of the embryo Dane and a nameless moorland tributary. In this romantic home of the red grouse, surrounded by high heather-clad hills, and adorned with many a miniature Niagara and here and there a diminutive cannon, the fugitive, swindling Flash-man was wont, in old times, to evade the law officers of one county by the simple process of moving on into the next.

Flash is most law-abiding and agriculturally industrious to-

day; but, I am told, there are people still living in the neighbourhood who fancy that the authorities of, say Stafford, are powerless to interfere with them for an offence committed in Derbyshire or Cheshire.

*W.H. Nithsdale*

## LEEK PAST AND PRESENT

Metropolis of the Moorlands,
Of thee we gladly speak;
Fair bulwark of our native land,
Hail! ancient town of Leek.

For centuries thy worthy fame
Has stood the test of time,
And Leke, or Leek, has been thy name
Since days of Auld Lang Syne.

What stirring scenes have taken place
In days of ancient yore,
It would, of course, take too much space
To con them fully o'er.

31

LEEK GRAMMAR SCHOOL

In days of old if dames grew warm,
The Churnet kept quite cool;
We hope it did their health no harm
Whilst in the ducking-stool.

The grumbling tongue might have a rest,
From angry language cease;
A time, at least, those they opprest
Might spend in quiet peace.

Perhaps the gents at times, as well,
Deserved a cooling bath,
Thus teaching them 'tis wise to dwell
In peace, avoiding wrath.

But now the ducking-stool and pranks
Are things of distant past;
Their services dispensed, with thanks,
They've long aside been cast.

In Leek did Johnson's father as
Apprentice serve his time
With Mr Joseph Needham learn
In Days of Auld Lang Syne.

Through Leek the young Pretender came
With his Scotch army past;
No doubt his visit and his name
O'er Leek a gloom would cast.

Leek had her own brave, noble sons,
And daughters, too, of old;
The deeds of many famous ones
Will often be re-told.

Now, gliding down to present times,
Leek friends we gladly greet;
In conversation or in rhymes
We're pleased with you to meet.

Your famous silk, may it be worn
By ladies, far and near;
The town and country well adorn,
Numbers in silk appear.

Your groceries and bread, and beef,
Right useful they are found;
Often affording much relief,
May customers abound.

LOADING STONE AT FROGHALL WHARF

The friends in Leek with pleasure see
Our country folks in town,
For they fresh eggs and butter need,
And cheese of good renown.

The farmers well enjoy a drive
Through country lanes to town,
They sometimes need a coat or vest,
Ladies require a gown.

From many miles around they come,
Some produce bring – to sell,
Others to look about them come,
And hear the news – or tell.

When driving home, the landscape fair
Stretching on either hand –
With gentle breeze and pure fresh air –
Attention doth demand.

Metropolis of the Moorlands,
The purest pleasures seek,
And find, and still in honour stand,
Fair favoured town of Leek.

*Alfred Hine*

## COAL MINES OF THE POTTERIES

Although the chief business of Hanley and Shelton in the past was the manufacture of earthenware and china, the wealth of coal beneath the town is very great. The pit shafts and air pits show how abundant the existence of mines has been, and how many places the surface mines have been worked. Writing sixty years ago, Mr Ward briefly referred to the late Earl Granville paying a large royalty to the Duchy of Lancaster for mine rent. Since that day the development and output have grown immensely. The Racecourse pits, which were commenced about 1870, at the rear of Etruria Hall have three large shafts, one of these being used for drawing water only. The depth of the workings for coal and ironstone is here 400 yards. This depth is reached in 18 strokes of the engine, the distance from surface to lowest workings being covered in about half a minute. The Deep Pit at Far Green is more than double the depth of the above-named, and nearly approaches 1,000 yards. These workings stretch some miles underground. As a matter of fact the miners get almost underneath Stoke on one hand, and on the other side to Foxley, near Milton. At Boothen, the bottom of Hope Street, there are three engines for pumping out the water from mines, one of which can dispose of six tons per minute.

Close to the Hanley Goods Station are the Slippery Lane and Rowhurst Pits, belonging the S.I.S. and C. (later Earl

NEWCASTLE UNDER LYME

Granville's). A large quantity of coals are obtained here for household and manufacturing purposes. The ironstone ore is obtained at a depth of about 300 yards, and is found in the Racecourse Pits, where are extensive hearths for calcining it. The local names of this ore are Pennistone, Gubbin, and Bassymine, and the minerals were much more used when those furnaces existed close to Bell's Mill.

No town has been more worked in the past for coals than Hanley, and of late we had some startling disasters. A man proceeding to his work early one December morning of 1904 had a terrible end. He was seen and spoken to by another, who then, fortunately, crossed over the road. Hearing a hollow sound as of something falling, he looked round, and to his horror beheld the one whom he had just saluted disappear from sight. On his turning to the spot he beheld a deep chasm, which was close to a doorstep in St John Street. The authorities, after this event, did their best to discover other shafts by probing in various places, and engaged a man who had been used to descending shafts, and had them filled up by his men. Since then Mr Robert S. Hastings has had a narrow escape in his stableyard, a shaft being, by him, staved in through moving a heavy packing case. On hearing the peculiar sound he found that he was on the brink of a pit 55 feet deep.

*William Scarratt*

## CHEADLE

At Cheadle, the principal event of the year has been the opening of the Town Hall, which has been erected at a total cost of about £4,000. Notwithstanding every effort of the local committee of the Cheadle Railway Company, the advancement of the line from Totmonslow has not yet been brought to a successful issue, but hopes are entertained now that the North Staffordshire Railway Company will seek Parliamentary powers to enable them to subscribe towards the project. The report of the tape and silk industries cannot be presented in rosy colours, although there has been an influx of weavers from Lancashire to work a large number of new tape looms imported by Messrs J. and N. Philips and Co. The arrival of these hands necessitated the erection of twenty new houses. Mining, which constitutes the chief industry of the neighbourhood, has been carried with the usual prosperity. Messrs Dickinson, Offer, and Co., who have commenced the sinking of a new shaft on the Draycott estate, have met with an unprecedented flow of water which has greatly impeded their progress.

*Staffordshire Advertiser,* 'Events 1894'

COAL DELIVERY, TOWN END, CHEADLE

## BASS'S BEER FRAUD

The tricks of trade are infinite. It is quite bad enough to play them with beer – say, of your own brewing – and to run risks of Excise visitation; but to palm off an inferior article under the name of 'Bass' is really too bad. It is rather an ingenious artifice to place genuine labels of the great Company upon bottles containing a totally different product of malt and hops, but it is a bolder stroke to put up a signboard, five feet by three, having on it the words, 'Bass and Co.'s Pale Burton Ales', and in the middle the well-known trade mark in the shape of a red triangle, and to supply a customer who asks for the genuine article with a beverage totally different from that demanded. That this was done we learn from proceedings the other day taken in Chancery Division of the High Court of Justice. Information of what the law is on the point cannot be too widely circulated, and we wish those publicans who are not quite so particular in their trading as they ought to be to take warning and avoid the scrape they would be liable to get into. In the Court two motions were made for injunctions to restrain two different sets of defendants from advertising, selling, or offering for sale beer which was represented as being brewed by Bass and Co., whereas it was nothing of the kind. Mr Decimus Sturges, Barrister-at-Law, appeared for the plaintiffs. The defendants were Messrs. Wakley and Fanshawe, carrying on business at three public-houses, the Ben Jonson (Harrow-road), the Wheatsheaf (Edgeware-road), and the Hall Arms (Church-street). The report of the proceedings does not divulge the mode of trading complained of, therefore we are

OPENING NEW HADEN COLLIERY, CHEADLE

WORTHINGTON'S BREWERY, BURTON ON TRENT

WOLSTANTON

DUDLEY STREET, WOLVERHAMPTON

ignorant of the gravity of the beer, and equally so as to the gravity of the offence; but we must state to the credit of the defendant firm that they met the case fairly, put no impediment in the way, and at once consented to the injunction in the terms asked for, and also to an inquiry into the profits and damages sustained by the plaintiffs, although it was set forth that the object of the proceedings is not for the mere amount of damages or profit, but to restrain the defendants and others who might do the same thing. Accidents will happen in the best regulated public-houses, and we are not going to hint or suggest a word beyond this. It is clear that the plaintiffs were justified in their proceedings; it is equally clear that the defendants acted wisely in submitting as they did. Thus ends case No. 1. No. 2 was somewhat more romantic. The individual complained of was George Endox, of the Oxford Arms, Westminster Bridge-road. He is the party who had outside his house the signboard above referred to. On a particular day the plaintiff sent two persons to the public-house, and they took with them two clean stone jars. They asked first for a pot of Bass's bitter beer, which was drawn and put into one of the jars; and then they asked for a pot of Bass's Burton beer, and that was drawn into the other jar. The two jars were then firmly sealed up and taken away

for the purposes of analysis direct to the analyst of the firm, who stated that he opened the jar labelled 'Bass's Burton, Oxford Arms, 8d.', and analysed part of its contents, which he found of high colour, flat, and of aërated character. The original gravity was 86.1, and the quantity of sulphuric anhydride as sulphates was 48 grains per gallon. From these numbers he was able to state positively that the beer was not Bass's Burton ale, nor was it any price ale of their brewing. He also opened the jar labelled 'Bass's Bitter, Oxford Arms, 6d.', and analysed part of its contents, which he found flat, aërated, and pale. The original gravity was 54.7, and the quantity of sulphuric anhydride as sulphates was 36 grains per gallon. From these numbers he was able to state positively that the beer was not Bass's pale ale, nor was it any price ale of their brewing. What was complained of was the abuse of the plaintiff's name and trade-mark, and it was asked that the injunction might be granted. The defendant appeared in person, and stated that he could not afford to pay counsel; his was a very small house, and he did very little business. He had, however, written an apologetic letter, stating that the signboard was on the house when he took it ten years ago, and had never been renewed, but only washed and revarnished, and that it was a copy of the plaintiff's bottle label; that if the

BASS'S HOP STORE, BURTON ON TRENT

plaintiffs insisted, he would have it painted out or altered; that he deeply regretted that any member of his family should have supplied ale that professed to be of the plaintiff's brewing; and that he would pledge his word that such a thing should not occur again. The defendant, judging from his statement to the court, appeared not quite to realise his position. He said that the beer sold as that of the plaintiff's was done so without his knowledge, and that his barmaid had sold it; but he was not, for a moment, prepared to contradict the evidence. Then he asked the question whether he was to understand that this injunction was to compel him not to sell Bass's ale in any shape or form. His Lordship answered: 'Not at all; you may sell Bass's ale, but it must be Bass's. What you sold was some other beer, and sold it as Bass's. You may sell as much as you like of Bass's, and I dare say the plaintiffs will be glad for you to sell large quantities.' It was also explained to him that, although he made an apology to the plaintiffs, they were not bound to accept it. The injunction was to restrain him until the trial of the action pending against him, but if he submitted now he would simply have the costs up to that day to pay, and avoid any further costs. The injunction was granted, the defendant being left to his meditations whether he would act wisely by adopting his lordship's suggestion, which, for his own sake, we doubt not he will see the propriety of doing.

We have not felt disposed to comment upon either of the

above cases with any great degree of severity, mainly by reason of the submissions made; there was practically no defence, or one that could, indeed, be offered; the parties were caught, and they were wise in making the best of a bad job. It must not be concluded, however, that we treat the matter lightly. Indeed, we do not. We really regard it seriously. The injury is primarily to the great name and high reputation of Bass, and, secondarily, to that portion of the public, by no means an unimportant one, who wish to drink the beer of the great Burton Company. Therefore, in the interests of the public, quite as much as in their own, Bass and Co. naturally feel compelled to take proceedings whenever such facts are brought to their notice as these we have alluded to.

*Licensed Victualler's Gazette and Hotel Courier, November 15 1898*

## THE MOST HOPS IN THE WORLD

The hop store in Messrs Bass's Brewery is said to be the largest in any brewery in the world. It is a detached three-storeyed brick building, 600 feet long, 140 feet wide, which was erected in the year of 1865. Mr Cooke, the manager of the department, was our guide, and humorously informed us that

BASS'S BARLEY STORE, BURTON ON TRENT

this unique building was fifty feet longer and wider than Noah's Ark, and produced his Bible to prove it. If this be the case, and we do not doubt it, Noah's shipwrights must have been clever builders, to be able to put together such a huge floating house, the height of which was 55 feet. As we approached the building, Mr Cooke pointed out the arrangement of this vast edifice. The basement and sub-basement are used for storage of ale, and the entire top storey, two acres in extent, for hops. We ascended one long flight of steps inside the house to reach the latter place, and, after resting a few moments in the head storekeeper's office, we proceed to explore the wonders of this store. When the building was first erected the whole area before us was an entire floor, but the Insurance Company stepped in, and according to their rules, which regulate the policies, the firm divided it into two large rooms by a hollow brick wall 2 feet thick; the opening, or communication between them, being by an outside iron balcony. These two rooms are sub-divided by wooden partitions into several parts, and are used as receiving-rooms, offices, weighing room, and storerooms. The hops are landed in six cages, attached to the receiving-rooms by an endless band driven by the engines, which drive a couple of shafts the whole length of the building on either side, raising not only the hops but the ale to the stores as stated. As the pockets are landed, they are wheeled off by the

hop-men, on jiggers, into a long side room, every pocket being weighed and a sample taken from it on its arrival. In the weighing room adjoining, the hops are afterwards blended and weighed daily into quantities ready for the coppers in the various breweries, each large bag being duly labelled and its weight tabulated. The apartment at the front of the building is divided or marked off for convenience sake, and the name of the brewery painted on the walls, and when the hops have been thus blended and weighed by the respective brewers, they are placed in divisions for immediate use and lowered into floaters for delivery to the three breweries.

On leaving this place, we entered the north store room and found ourselves almost in total darkness, but, at the word of command from Mr Cooke, the clerk in the office turned up the gas, and we obtained a view of this vast store. From all the rooms where the hops are stored, the daylight is religiously excluded, as also draught. The hops must, however, always be kept cool and dry, and to this end there is a double ceiling in the roof of the building, formed by boards tongued and grooved together, fixed 9 inches from the roof, giving a current of air in the space thus formed.

As we progressed through the series of rooms, countless piles of hop-pockets from floor to ceiling stared in our faces or towered by our side, and the aroma was almost overpowering.

The weekly consumption of hops in the company's three

ALLSOP'S BREWERY, BURTON ON TRENT

breweries is now about sixty tons, but as many as seventy-four tons have been used in a busy week. On glancing at the figures in the hop store-books we found that the annual consumption for a decade of years amounted to 33,458 cwts, representing a money value of £267,664 per annum.

The arrangements for extinguishing fire in this department are most perfect and complete. There are eight hydrants on the walls, and fire plugs in enclosed boxes springing from the floor at intervals of a few yards throughout the building, are connected with the water mains from the tower. Apart from the company's regular fire brigade, Mr Cooke has a trained hop-store brigade, which includes twenty of his own hop-men, himself the chief. As we were retracing our steps to his office, and without any warning to us, he suddenly pulled the fire signal to show us the efficiency of his men. In less than two-and-a-half minutes every man in the place had left his work and was in our apartment, each with his roll of hose on his back or grenade in his hand. The signal had been given that the fire had broken out in the central store, and thither the men had raced as fast as they could, ready to do their duty. Before our voices could reach them, they had detached the hose and turned on the cocks, and we then expressed regret that we had been the cause of playing them such a trick, to which our guide replied, 'It is good practice for them.'

*Alfred Barnard*

## RANGEMORE HALL

As soon as we reached the 'Beer City', we found an invitation for us to visit Rangemore, the seat of Lord Burton, distant some six or seven miles. Having a keen relish for the pleasures and employments of country life, and loving the beauties of nature with the intensity and enthusiasm of those in city pent, this was rare good news for us, and we were right glad to break loose from our studies to take a drive along country roads and green lanes to the uplands of Needwood Forest. We were a party of three, and, to our infinite satisfaction, we found an open carriage had been provided for us. A bright blue sky was overhead, and the sun was pouring down its golden rays on hill and dale when we started, as merry a party as ever revelled in a summer's day. After leaving the suburb of Shobnall, the route began to ascend, and our way for several miles lay along country roads, here and there bordered with banks covered with bushes, tumbling about in all directions, encroaching where they liked, sometimes almost even with the footpaths; presently, we came to hedgerows covered with wild roses and creeping plants, cut off from our track by ditches filled with swarthy growth and tall wild flowers. Then we passed openings to country lanes, whose thick hedges were covered with blackberries; anon we got peeps into thick copses, where the hazel boughs were covered with ripening nuts. Soon we came to a farmhouse, and saw beyond fields, fertile in corn and other life-supporting produce of the earth. The district through which we passed does not abound in

THE HAPPY COUPLE, RUDYARD

STAFFS AND WORCS CANAL, COMPTON

grand and sublime prospects, but home scenes of rural repose and sheltered nooks are plentiful. The road was continually winding past old farm-houses and labourers' cottages, and our eyes were constantly captivated by a continual succession of small landscapes of delightful loveliness. On arriving at the margin of Needwood Forest the road turned to the left, passing by a portion of the estate belonging to Mr Hamar A. Bass, MP, and very soon after this we reached our destination.

The mansion-house of Rangemore, which is a modern building, is situated on a pleasant slope, environed by thick groves of trees, fruit gardens, and several acres of hot-houses, and we did not see it until we were just upon it. This, we think, is best; because, if a place is visible some miles distant, it seems unaccountably long before one reaches it, especially if it stands on an elevation and the surrounding country is level. Rangemore cannot be complained of in this respect, for it hides itself most cunningly in the trees that obscure it from view, and, it was not until we came to a sudden turn of the road in the grounds, that we found ourselves almost within a few yards of it. It was at this point that we left the carriage and walked to the terrace in front of the house to get a sight of the valley which stretches out before it. The mansion stands on an extensive and magnificent lawn, sloping down to the edge of a pretty lake like a carpet of green velvet, studded and enamelled with beds of flowers, almost too beautiful to look upon except

on Sundays or holidays. The nice distribution of flowers and plants of tender and graceful foliage, the slopes of velvet turf, the silver gleam of water through the trees, all denote the master hand of Sir Joseph Paxton, the king of landscape gardeners, who has here given us a specimen of his unrivalled skill, and whose genius has made of the Rangemore gardens and conservatories a veritable paradise. The park encloses within it, on a small scale, every diversity of miniature hill and dale, and, everywhere, displays the soft grace of a fertile country. After admiring the prospect, we descended the slopes to the valley below and commenced our explorations. From this point, we had a perfect view of the house and grounds, with their lovely surroundings, which consist chiefly of low hills covered with woods and groves, redolent in beauty. On one side rises a thick wooded hill, the trees presenting the richest and most variegated foliage, on the other, green and luxuriant grassy slopes, covered with clumps of shrubs in every variety. Here and there, after we had passed to the other side of the lake, the trees receded and formed little amphitheatres of beauty; sometimes the path descended and we came to the water's edge, when we made the acquaintance of graceful swans, some of them jet black, which came swimming towards us; presently, the path pursued its way amid the trees, and we passed a range of pens or large cages wherein are imprisoned a number of Tartarian pheasants, eagles, and other wild birds.

BROOK FARM, PERRY BARR

Continuing our walk we reached the reservoir or dam, entirely hidden by trees, which feeds the lake, where all kinds of waterfowl, including seagulls, take shelter.

Leaving this, we visited the gardens, stored with every vegetable production, next the orchards pendant with their beauteous burden, and then passed through the numerous hothouses filled with grapes, figs, melons, pines, peaches and apricots. As we descended from the terrace on which these gardens are planted, the sunbeams glittered upon long ranges of those fragile buildings, which luxury has invented to outwit nature, and, although, our time was somewhat limited, we could not resist the temptation of a promenade through them. It would be impossible for us to describe the beauty and rarity of their contents. Choice orchids, tropical flowers, and carnations as big as dahlias stared us in the face, filling the air with their perfumes. Rare exotics, rich foliage and delicate ferns were in magnificent profusion, and, in each house, creepers and hanging plants of every hue and variety depended from the roof. On leaving the conservatories, we proceeded to the Hall, where we partook of a sumptuous luncheon, and afterwards made a tour of the place. All the apartments are large and lofty, and contain a choice collection of paintings and water colours; every available space, even to the halls and passages, being covered with valuable works of art, which it is Lord Burton's delight to collect. As the family were leaving the next day for Scotland, we did not see very much of the furniture and rare articles of *vertu* which the house possesses, as they were mostly shrouded or in the process of being covered up. We were, however, shown the bedroom occupied by the

TUTBURY CASTLE

BLACKSMITH HENRY RODEN, PENN

late Michael Thomas Bass and in which he died; also the adjoining apartment wherein he transacted his correspondence; both are plainly but substantially furnished, and everything has been left untouched, even to the pictures on the walls, which consist mostly of portraits of the friends of the illustrious gentleman. The billiard-room, the largest and most notable apartment in the house, is evidently much used, particularly in summer, as it combines both a morning and writing room. The recesses of the deep windows, which overlook the grounds on both sides of the house, are the favourite haunts of guests, as they form quiet nooks for correspondence. As we wished to see the church and hamlet of Rangemore, which are situated in the direction of the homeward route, we now took our departure, making a circuit of the splendid stables and coach-houses before resuming our carriage. They are well worth seeing, being substantially and artistically built; the whole of the interior walls of the stables are lined with coloured tiles; the woodwork being all of teak and the whole place fitted up with every requisite appliance, which we would describe did space permit. A path, called the Church walk, leads from the grounds to Rangemore church; it is bordered by a lawn, on which is planted, on either side,

beautiful trees and shrubs of almost every variety.

The church, which stands in the centre of the hamlet, is a handsome edifice with a graceful spire, the top of which can be seen for many miles round. It was built by the late Mr Michael Thomas Bass, whose remains rest in a simple grave in the churchyard, near the window of the chancel. Since his decease, another aisle has been added by his son, Lord Burton, 'in loving memory of his father', in which several memorial windows, rich in tracery and painted glass, have been placed by Mrs Bass, her son Mr H.A. Bass, M.P., and her two daughters. From the church, we walked to the village school and literary institute, both the gifts of Lord Burton; the latter contains, besides a reading room and library, a capital billiard room.

*Alfred Barnard*

## NELLIE BASS'S WEDDING

Miss Bass's wedding to Mr Baillie of Dochfour was the event not only of this week but of the winter. The daughter of Lord

NELLIE BASS AT RANGEMORE, BURTON ON TRENT

Burton is the richest heiress in England, and, being popular in herself as well as important in her position, it was natural that she should be inundated with unusually valuable presents. As a matter of fact, these exceeded by some 200 the number (400) which it is the ambition of every bride to attain.

The weather on the wedding-day was so far favourable that, having rained intermittently all morning, it cleared about two o'clock, and there was not even a shower until the ceremony was over. The bride's gown, a masterpiece of Mrs Mason's, was the richest white satin, fitting her so well that she looked taller and thinner than she really is. At the feet it was embroidered lightly with pearl wheat-ears; at the waist it was simply girdled with ribbons; at the throat there was a frill of Brussels point – such a frill as Mrs Langtry is seen wearing in so many of her photographs – and this, lying at the base of her throat, allowed her beautiful dog-collar, a big curb-chain of brilliants, to be seen. In the front of her bodice she wore a curved star of diamonds, given her by Lady Burton; and two beautiful bracelets (one of which had a button pearl surrounded by brilliants as a centre, while the other had a

triple cluster) were shown to best advantage, as she wore no gloves, and her transparent Brussels-lace sleeves only reached a little lower than the elbow. Her bare right hand was covered with rings, amongst them her engagement ring of rubies and diamonds. She wore a golden lucky-bell among the ribbons at her wrist, and you could actually hear it tinkling as she moved. Her bridesmaids were ten in number. As they all stood near the entrance of the church waiting for the bride they made a charming group. Their frocks were white satin, edged with inch wide beaver; a frill of cream lace that edged the yoke fell over mauve chiffon, and mauve chiffon also edged the frills at the waist. The big violet velvet hats were trimmed with shaded violets and plumes of black feathers (black is supposed to be lucky at a wedding); and their bouquets were of violets – dark purple and pale – with lilies-of-the-valley.

Chesterfield House, which is an historic mansion, looked its very best on the occasion of the wedding. The beautiful marble staircase is a feature of the house, and above it hung a portrait of Miss Bass, full length, with a fur-trimmed cloak falling off her shoulders, a wedding present from Miss Baillie.

Everywhere were palms and flowers. The bride and bridegroom received in the drawing-room, the presents were displayed in the big ballroom, and refreshments were served in both dining-rooms.

Most beautiful among the wedding gifts was the pearl-and-diamond tiara which was to have belonged to the future Queen of England, the young Duchess of York. The diamonds are very large, and the pearl points are nearly an inch deep. Altogether, anything handsomer could scarcely be imagined. To wear with it there was a necklace formed of a double row of single-stone diamonds in front, while a single row of pearls fastens it behind. This fashion of having pearls at the back of a necklace is evidently popular. Mrs Ratcliff's necklace of diamonds and rubies had three handsome pendants, and the back was a plain row of pearls. The turquoise-and-diamond coronet, given by her father, is made in big clusters, and another given her by Mrs Arthur James is very similar. The diamond curb chain which the bride wore at the wedding was the gift of Mr Baillie. It fitted the throat like a collar, and the links were so large that the throat was practically bare. The diamond necklace given by the townspeople of Burton was also very much admired. A number of people gave the bride jewelled pins, which are now so much used for scarf-ties and for hats. A beautiful glove-box from Lady de Trafford was oblong and made of turquoise blue velvet, with 'Nellie' written in diamonds upon it. Mr Berkeley Levett gave a small heart-shaped patch-box of tortoiseshell, and this also had the bride's name upon it. A paper-knife similarly adorned was

quite half a yard in length, made of a very fine piece of solid tortoiseshell. Some of the little boxes were made more beautiful by miniatures, and a number of presents, including those from the Duke of Marlborough, Lord Rowton, and Lady Brougham, were antiques. All the wedding presents were laid upon red damask, which covered the impromptu tables ranged all round the big ballroom. At the end of the room where the windows face the Park was the presentation plate – a magnificent mass! In fact, the silver was more admired than the jewels. The presents given by the Duke and Duchess of Fife were two small bangles, one set with rubies and diamonds, the other set with diamonds and sapphires. The fan given by the Duchess of York was white and spangled with silver. Among the things that pleased the bride most were the little thoughtful presents given by the tenants and village people round about Dochfour, Rangemore, and Glenquoich, many of them trifles, such as pen-wipers, pin-cushions, &c., but all valued as tributes of the esteem in which bride and bridegroom are both held where best known.

*Staffordshire Advertiser February, 3 1894*

## THE GILBERT CHARITY

'The old folks' treat' is annually looked forward to by those to whom a feast comes rarer than a fast. The founder of the feast was Mr Thomas Gilbert. In appearance stout, rubicund, and

HORSE FAIR, RUGELEY

of medium height, with a peculiar turn in his eye when smiling – he was the soul of fun. He confessedly owned to being a 'bon vivant',told tales so quaintly that he could keep a company in laughter for a long time. For some years he was a borough rate collector of Hanley continuing so till his death. As he thought nothing could surpass the experiences of the Epicure, he left all his money, it is said, for an annual feed to those who could best appreciate it – the poor.

*William Scarratt*

## THE BEAUTY OF RUGELEY

Those who visit the town of Rugeley for the first time cannot fail to be struck by the brightness and beauty of its surroundings – supposing of course the day to be a fine one. Few towns retain their native cheerfulness in bad weather, and Rugeley would not desire for one moment to be an exception to the general rule. The visitor, however, in order to ensure obtaining a good impression of the town should alight from the train at the Trent Valley Station, when the sky is bright and the sun is shining, and as he places his foot upon the platform and turns his face towards the town, he cannot but admire the view which meets his gaze. Straight before him, as he casts a glance over the smiling valley beneath, his eyes rest upon the long ridge of hills – the famous Cannock Chase –

with the beacon-like Etching hill in the foreground, with its flagstaff and grassy slopes. Behind is the level line of the Chase, while to the left is to be discerned the lofty and more wooded summit of Stile Cop. Further to the left the view becomes more picturesque, the high hills in the vicinity of Brereton Colliery, and on towards Longdon, being gradually hidden by the woods which finally close in the prospect. Then the eye turns to the valley, the wide sweep of pasture land in each direction, and the winding Trent flowing from right to left, increasing the fertility of the country around and the beauty of the view. If the visitor, however, be in a hurry, and anxiously looks about for the town itself, he can see but little of it, so hidden is it by the luxuriant growth of foliage, and the tall trees which protect it from the vulgar gaze. The fact, however, that the town actually lies in that direction is rendered apparent by the presence of the two square towers belonging to the old and new parish churches, and the elegant and graceful spire of the Roman Catholic Church. The old church tower is almost hidden behind its leafy screen, while the more modern tower, being loftier, becomes a more prominent object. The tower of the Town Hall is also just discernable, but beyond a few houses on the outskirt of the town there is nothing more to show that Rugeley lies in that direction. A winding roadway from the railway station leads by a new bridge over the river and past a mill, passing between green hedges, until it reaches the canal and the parish church. If the visitor looks to the right, he perceives that the country

ST PETER'S SQUARE, WOLVERHAMPTON

CHUBB'S LOCK FACTORY, WOLVERHAMPTON

becomes more thickly wooded in the direction of Stafford, and that the line of railway at last becomes lost in the distance. The view is, altogether, one of the prettiest to be imagined, and the visitor must be very indifferent to the charms of nature if he fails to bestow upon it befitting admiration.

*Alfred Williams*

## LOCKS AND CORRUGATED IRON

Wolverhampton makes locks, the chief works being those of Messrs Chubb, who are known the world over.

Chubbs make every lock by hand, and no two locks exactly alike; and they have one man who examines every lock they make at three different stages, so as to ensure its being correct in workmanship and action. The narrow rooms of what was once the old workhouse are crowded with men, each at his bench, some of them having been in their employ for years, including the seven during which the firm removed to London, and had to return for want of locksmiths. In these days of cast-iron cases and ill-tempered springs, it is a relief to come across a lock that is mostly of brass throughout and is really built to last. It seems strange that so simple a thing as the case of a lock should be shaped and made by hand, but so it is. Orders in this trade run into long numbers, orders for prisons,

for ships, for hotels, in addition to the everyday house and office work, every lock made to fit the key, which is generally of brass for Indian and tropical climates.

If locks go all over the world, so does galvanised iron; and Wolverhampton has been making galvanised iron ever since it was invented. This is a very different sort of industry, and requires much space and division of labour. The Wolverhampton Corrugated Iron Company occupies ten acres, and is known in almost every foreign and colonial port. And the peculiarities of every port have to be studied. If you send corrugated iron to Australia, you pack it in cases, for Australia has railway trucks to carry it inland; if you sent it to South Africa, you pack it in bundles with felt, for thus only can it be carried in bullock waggons; if you send it to Central America, it must be in single sheets, for thus only can it be carried on mule-back.

*Midland Sketches, 1898*

## SPELLING BEES

Much amusement and instruction was caused, about 1870, by an American entertainment called 'Spelling Bees'. At the first Spelling Bee in the Potteries, given in the Large Lecture Hall, at the Mechanics' Institution, the place was packed, many

STAFFS AND WORCS CANAL, NEWBRIDGE

coming from a distance. Unusual words, and those whose phonetic sounds gave little indication of how they were spelt (omitting those pertaining to the sciences), were selected. It was amusing to see the disappointment of those who failed. This kind of entertainment only lasted for a year or two.

The second Spelling Bee in Hanley had been better thought out. The difficult words were arranged in progressive order, and small cards, on which the words were written, were placed before the interrogator, so that even he could not unfairly use a selection. The following sentence broke down even the first prize winner:– 'A phthisical patient suffering from inflammation of the lungs applied to a pharmaceutical chemist for a phial of ipecacuanha wine.'

*William Scarratt*

## CANAL SIDE DRAMA

The weather gods have been good to us for Friday brought another ideal morning. Dad and I, after dreaming of the Manifold, were both late for breakfast; and it was half-past nine by the time we cycled off Southbank into the road for Cheddleton and Cheadle. We took the pace leisurely; walked up Cheddleton Heath, and stopped for a glance at the canal life at Cheddleton.

'We're going down this Churnet Valley, are we not, Nithsdale?' Dad queried as we watched a gorgeously decorated barge through the locks.

'Aye'.

'There's no road between here and Oakamoor you say?'

'No'.

'Why not take the tow-path?'

'Because the railway company forbids bicycles.'

'Rubbish! You've been along many a time, I'll bet.'

'I have, but —'

'Oh, come on. There will be fewer of your banks to climb.'

'All right then. But mind you, Wilkie, you'll have to pay the fines.'

Without further ado we commenced our trespass.

The going was not exactly all one could wish, neither was our Indian file particularly sociable; but the spice of danger

ELFORD

with the canal so close, the Churnet unprotected on our left, and a possibility of trouble with the railway company, made the ride sufficiently fascinating. Beyond the paper mill the path narrowed, and our pleasures were increased by the necessity of dismounting to pass a boat horse.

Basford Bridge, a small hamlet, with Cheddleton Station and its pretty buildings, are worthy a passing note. I would here remark on the tasteful designs of all the North Stafford station architecture we have seen. Beyond Basford Bridge, where the Churnet Valley is open and picturesque, the path was more comfortable both in surface and width. We thoroughly enjoyed the unpremeditated deviation from the beaten track, and the occasional barge we met or passed added materially to the interest of the run; although I always felt a trifle nervous when pushing past a steadily plodding pony.

At the second lock below Basford Bridge, the Churnet Lock, our host told us of an experience he had with an inebriated lady bargee, who by carelessness had contrived to sink her craft in the lock.

She was a smart plucky little woman, who, aided by a willing horse while her lord was drinking at Cheddleton, had navigated the barge single handed to Froghall; had shipped a cargo; got through the Froghall tunnel, and was well on her way back. She would have done well enough had she refrained from the spirituous consolation she carried in a black bottle. Our host and a friend, seeking pictures along the bank, fell in with her above Froghall, and as they proceeded alongside she shipped them as crew, without wages, to drive the now refractory animal. They soon tired of the job and discharged themselves; in consequence of which and their refusal to photograph a pet canary, there were words. Words which increased in bitterness each time the parties met in their peregrinations. The voyage was most eventful. Twice the lady was shipwrecked, and each time had to impose upon the good nature of the crews of passing craft, the latter of whom left the lock open for her.

While waiting for a suitable light in the immediate neighbourhood they were startled by piercing shrieks; and on running to the lock saw the nose of the heavily laden barge caught under the lock gate. The screaming, half-drunken Amazon had sense sufficient to close the lock paddles; but too late. The waters rose rapidly above the load line, on the decks, and then rushed in a series of falls into the cabins and the hold. The 'Stanley' foundered in a few seconds, leaving

51

BURTON ON TRENT

nothing but the aft cabin deck, and the plank lines of communication between stem and stern, above the water.

After silently contemplating the scene for a while the lady remembered her canary. She turned appealingly to them and asked if one would go down the ten feet of lock to rescue the bird. 'No fear,' said our host ungallantly; but he added had it been a baby he would not have minded getting wet. At a paltry canary, however, certainly drowned by this time, he rigidly drew a line. The lady became hysterical: alternately she screamed, beseeched and swore; until eventually, on the assurance that he could reach the cage without getting wet, he tumbled on to the cabin deck below. But he found he could not even see the cage; and as he positively declined to go into the submerged cabin, the lady, to his astonishment, came down beside him. She was in the water before he could stop her, and when he caught her she fought like a wild cat. But presently, sobered by the water, she recognised the futility of the struggle and adopted beseeching tactics. Holding her by the wrist he let her into the cabin, which had but a foot of air space, to where she reached that canary. And now he swears the miserable bird never had its feet wet until it was pulled through the water. The excitement did not cease even then. The lady had to be assisted, by means of a rope and plank, up the ten feet of wall to the tow-path. There was more sport

when she wanted to go back again for dry clothes.

And finally after all this devotion to the bird, the brute of a husband in his passion on seeing his sunken ship, threw canary and cage into the middle of the canal.

*W.H. Nithsdale*

## THE NORKIES

The majority of the East Anglians who went up to Burton before the First World War were young, unmarried horsemen, young farm-workers who tended their horses and took them out to plough. Some of them described the conditions in Suffolk when they first went up. Albert George Ablett (born 1885) of Sibton Green, Suffolk, first went to Burton in 1903:

'There were about twenty young chaps without work in one small village like ours. It used to be that when the thrashing tackle came round they'd be going around asking for jobs a month or two before the machine actually got to the farm; and then of course they'd be denied. There weren't nobody a-doing nawthen, hardly. They wouldn't even pay the money to cut the bushes back. The farms were neglected. I mean you'd got big owd fences. Some on 'em would take up

BURTON ON TRENT

half the field – left, you know. They wouldn't pay anyone to do it. The fences all grown up like woods. They use to grow each side of the road till they met, you know.'

John Dennis Kettle (born 1894) of Framsden first went to Burton in 1912. The conditions in the villages were still the same then:

'I was brought up in Earl Soham, and there were about fifty of us young chaps in that area without work after harvest. Farming was in a bad way. You couldn't get work only at haysel and harvest. The farmers didn't want you after the corn-harvest. They'd keep the married men on and the younger workers were laid off.'

'Well, I was lucky. I was a horseman and I niver had to lose time through bad weather. But my brother lived along o' me and I seen him come hoom on Saturday nights and give my mother five shillings. That's all he'd 'arned in the week! And he'd look at these five shillings and say: "Well, Mother, I'm a-going to git a red coat. I'm going to 'list." I sometimes used to go down to Cretingham *Bell*, and I say to him, "Come and have a pint, Arnie"; and he'd come down and have to change a two-shilling bit. So I suppose he find two bob somewhere. Poor owd Mother used to give it to him. So he didn't go and 'list. But he went up to Burton – him and his mate; and he came home 'arly in 1915 and joined up and went to Mesopotamia. He got killed in September 1918. And my mother niver had a medal for him. Niver found out anything about it, but of course she got a pension.'

LONGTON

53

'NORKIES', MALTSTERS FROM EAST ANGLIA

FIRST DAY OF TRAMS, BURTON ON TRENT

At the end of August and the beginning of September the Burton brewers sent agents down to various centres in East Anglia to engage the young farm-workers. Bass and Company sent a circular letter to each malting worker who had been employed during the previous season – if he had proved satisfactory.

Once the worker had signed on, the agent gave him a *single* railway ticket from the nearest railway station to Burton-on-Trent, and he went up on the following Monday. But as the villages were often a fair distance from the railway the men had to arrange to get to the station as best they could. Sam Friend recalled an occasion when he went up to Burton.

'A lot of us from round here went to Framlingham Station. Walter Mays used to keep a shop and he drove us down in his horse and trap. I went up on the 5th September and got on famously. But of course my mate had gone up the Monday afore. He came and met me at the station in Burton. Of course he'd got me lodgings next door to where he was lodging in Station Street. But I was telling you about the journey. There was one of the blokes who come with me from Cretingham in the horse and trap and he couldn't read nor write. So his mother gave him a postcard and say to him: "As soon as you get there do you post this. Then I'll know you're all right." Well, the fust thing he done when he got to

Framlingham station was to find a post-box and shove in the postcard to send to his mother. That's how we used to go on at that time o' day. But none of us had never been in a train afore. That was the fust time I went in a train when I went to Burton. And everything – the compartments and so on – were some strange.'

Sam Friend gave me an inkling of the impression this journey made on the young East Anglian workers by recounting two of its noteworthy points: 'When we came back home from Burton I recollect you could allus start an argument in a pub by saying outright: "I've seen 'em a-cutting wheat in March!" Of course, they wouldn't believe that, and there'd be bets and arguments. You could pick up a pint as easy as winking because when you came to prove it you could say that when you went to Burton last September the train passed through the Fens, and alongside the town of March you saw 'em a-cutting wheat. But you couldn't play that trick often.' And more seriously: 'Going up to Burton by train they used to say: "There ain't no Sundays once you've passed Leicester corner." You were going into a seven-day week and you couldn't tell a Sunday from a weekday.'

The same recruiting organization obtained in Norfolk, as Albert Love of Wortwell recalls: 'A number of young men used to go up to Burton at the beginning of the century;

ABBOT'S BROMLEY

though my father had been and lived up there I niver went up myself. They came from all the surrounding villages and they all came together at Homersfield station like soldiers and they went up to Burton together.

*George Ewart Evans*

[*Although migrant workers came to Burton from Suffolk and Norfolk they were all dubbed 'Norkies' by Burton people.*]

## OLD HOBB

An old custom still survives in Abbot's Bromley, known as the hobby horse dance, which formerly took place about Christmas time – some say at Easter or Whitsuntide, but which is now observed on the Wakes Monday every year. According to one historian: 'On this occasion a person danced through the principal street, carrying between his legs the figure of a horse composed of thin boards. In his hands he bore a bow and arrow, which last entered a hole in the bow, and stopping on a shoulder made a sort of snapping noise as he drew it to and fro, keeping time to the music. Five or six other individuals danced along with this person, each carrying on his shoulder six reindeer heads, three of them painted white,

and three red, with the arms of the chief families who had, at different times, been proprietors of the manor, painted on the palms of them.' Another historian says that the number of dancers was about a dozen, and that the arms consisted of those belonging to the families of Paget, Bagot and Welles, to whom the chief property of the town belonged. Dr Plott, in 1686, says: 'To this hobby horse dance there also belonged a pot which was carried by turns by four or five of the chief of the town who provided cakes and ale to put into it. All the people who had any kindness for the good interest of the institution of the sport gave pence apiece for themselves and families, as also the foreigners who came to see it, with which money the charge of the cakes and ale being defrayed, they not only repaired their church, but kept their poor,' 'which charges,' shrewdly adds the Doctor, 'are not now perhaps so cheerfully borne.' This practice is said to have existed in other places, being frequently mentioned in the old parish books of Stafford and Seighford. Degge says that something of the same kind was practiced at Stafford in order to obtain money for the repair of the church. Some of their chief inhabitants undertook to collect money from their friends, and whosoever brought in the greatest sum to the hobby horse was considered the man of best credit, so that each strove who should most improve his interest, and it was accounted for at Christmas. The custom, as it existed at Stafford, is said to have taken the

HORN DANCE, ABBOT'S BROMLEY

form of a procession, in which a wooden horse, gaily decorated with ribbons, formed the chief attraction. This was accompanied by music and morrice dancers, who begged from door to door. 'Old Hobb', a terrible figure, made with the scull of a horse, and drapery covering a man who worked the jaws, was a formidable object in the procession. Similar processions were prevalent in other parts of the country, from an early date, but the origin of this peculiar custom is shrouded in obscurity. The observance, so far as Abbot's Bromley was concerned, continued until the time of the Civil War between the Parliament and the Stuarts, when the inhabitants had something more weighty and serious to engage their attention. It was subsequently revived, and the horses and deer horns are still preserved in the tower of the parish church.

*Alfred Williams*

## LEEK MARKET DAY

By half-past nine our host had us down the town for the early arrivals – the butchers, cattle dealers, farmers, and cattle – in the Cattle Market; and some funny specimens of both man and animal we saw. Every man seemed to me to be armed with a stick, and when he had not both hands in his pockets with the stick at ease under his arm, he was belabouring some poor inoffensive beast. Ever and anon we came across a man, now coaxing, now pulling, now shoving, and occasionally bodily carrying a refractory calf. We saw sheep driven in and brought by cart, pigs in traps and floats, and once in a while were alarmed by a rushing avalanche of potential beef, behind which were several shouting, gesticulating, stick-carrying creatures such as in calmer moments might pass for men. It was a veritable pandemonium, but as yet only in embryo.

Turning into the town we saw all manner of vehicles, some smart and up-to-date, some middle-aged but serviceable, and some, relics of remote antiquity, venerable ramshackles; drawn by as many varieties of the genus gee-gee, and laden with a human freight as heterogeneous and even more picturesque.

The normal condition of Leek is decidedly dull and sleepy. Except at noon or at night, when the mill hands are abroad, its main thoroughfares are comparatively deserted. But this weekly Wednesday market brings a transformation. It is *the* day of the week: a day of bustle and activity, brimful of incident,

LEEK

and one which makes regular life here tolerable. Leek's is one of those old-world old-fashioned markets, attended by old-world old-fashioned people, which the march of modern civilization, the railway train, the motor car, the electric tram, and the prospective airship will some day relegate to things of the past. And Leek's market, because of Leek's peculiar and practically isolated situation in a highland country, will be one of the last to go.

These picturesque, quaintly attired farm folk from adjacent and remote hill fastnesses, bring in butter, eggs, and poultry and other farm produce, and generally leave their vehicles in lines along the principal thoroughfares. They wage a continual warfare with the tradespeople for possession of the road space adjoining the causeway; and mingle with tradesmen and dealers, selling, buying, bartering, haggling and jostling all over the town.

It is interesting to observe the arrival of the carrier, and as market women and market baskets emerge from the interior of his 'bus, we marvel at its capacity. There are eggs and butter in the baskets, and hens and ducks in crates and boxes. Once in a while a chicken escapes. In the midst of the ensuing chase half a score of frantic young stock come careering from the cattle market and become hopelessly entangled among the crowd of men and women, market baskets and vehicles. A basket of eggs is upset: somebody in avoiding another cow backs into a horse and starts it on a pantomimic turn; a third cow knocks down a youngster, and a fourth seeks refuge from the turmoil in an adjacent shop. Dear, dear! What a heap of trouble can be caused by a fifteen-penny chicken!

The carrier, himself, is a man of many parts. He accepts all manner of commissions: selling eggs and butter and poultry, and purchasing all sorts of articles required by people of the moorlands who cannot attend the market. He will have a lawn mower for the parson; notices for the parish council; a repaired cornet for a village bandsman; cycle parts for a bicycling lass up country; a pair of spectacles for some old lady; a box from the station for a servant girl home for holidays; medicine for sick folk; quack remedies for the unwell, and bread, groceries, and other necessaries of life for many families; and, by the time he starts for home, a fair cargo of liquor in himself.

We worked our way through the dense crowd in the butter market, where, as in the poultry and cattle markets and all other town lands to which the market is exclusively confined, the local authority levies toll. We saw the baskets of butter and eggs, the prices of which of course vary accordingly to supply and demand and the time of year; but which are steadier now the women folk are provided with a sheltered market than when they had to stand in open streets in all weathers. And when eggs are scarce and butter going at a discount, the lady is sometimes sufficiently autocratic as to refuse eggs, unless the customer will take butter. The poultry market with its mainstay of hens and ducks, and fringe of pigeons, rabbits, guinea pigs and doves, was also interesting.

We visited the cattle market again. The dealing, with the coming and going, slapping of hands, confidential whisperings, and now and then 'two penn'orth', had a fascination for Dad. Then we saw an auction mart. A

WOLVERHAMPTON

frightened beast preceeded a lithe, energetic individual, armed with a seemingly animated ash-plant into the ring of stock buyers, and was kept on the move in the small area within by that ash-plant most assiduously applied.

'Ten, ten, ten; eleven, twelve, twelve-a-half; thank you, thirteen. Thirteen, thirteen, thirteen-ten, fourteen. A good coloury cow, guaranteed sound. I've fourteen pounds bid. Fourteen offered; thank you, fourteen-five, fourteen-ten. Fourteen-fifteen for you, sir? Fourteen-fifteen it is. Fifteen pounds. At fifteen pounds. Take her away. Have you all done? At fifteen pounds. Mr Farmer, fifteen pounds.' And the poor beast was chased away before the ash-plant, to make room for another which had already been brought up.

Leaving the cattle market we saw the quack doctor, busy as ever, still humbugging the folk into believing they suffer from every malady humanity is heir to, and putting forward a pill with more good medicinal qualities than there are ways to heaven. We saw other general attributes. Cheapjacks, selling fancy hardware at fancy prices, for the mere advertisement: they are always advertising some American firm – with goods

made in Brum. The umbrella man, with a stock of gamps left in railway carriages: the dealer in second-hand brollies stocks most affectionately to the legend of the railway compartment. And in the Market Place among the stalls we heard tales of bankrupt stocks, soiled goods and faulty articles. 'Tis surprising how readily people will buy supposed indifferent goods when served with a shady reputation. The packman affects a sinister eloquence as he recites his doggerel tales of smuggling to ignorant housewives while unfolding the mysteries of his pack, which that very morning has been replenished in a perfectly legitimate manner in a warehouse in the same town.

Among the interesting out-door emporiums we noted those of the market gardeners – resplendent with blooming plants, butchers, fishmongers, grocers, greengrocers and drapers, and the usual itinerant booksellers, music vendors, tawdry jewellers, toffeemen and penny bazaars. There was a specialist in sewing machines, another in rubber stamps, and a knife grinder.

There was an outer circle of buskers, some giving quite a smart little entertainment before a crowd which rapidly

HORSEFAIR, LEEK

diminished on the approach of the hat; a sword swallower; a pavement artist; and a goodly array of the usual one-armed men, one-eyed men, one-legged men, men without legs and blind men.

*W.H. Nithsdale*

## A MAN WHO SOLD HIS ARM

All towns have their strange beings. In Tunstall, in the early fifties, a man could be seen who was a war veteran, and went under the cognomen of 'Waterloo', from having seen active service in that history-making battle. From being a soldier, he became a bricklayer's hodman. His peculiarity was an arm and hand covered with a mass of carunculus growth, familiarly known as warts. From the tops of his fingers to his elbow joint, leaving out the palm of his hand, the limb was literally covered with these small excrescences. On two occasions I was present when he bared his arm, and I also heard him say that he had sold the limb to Dr T——, a medical gentleman, for experimental purposes, for half-a-guinea, prepaid. The arm was to be disservered after his decease.

*William Scarratt*

## BASS'S TRIP TO YARMOUTH

### Warnings and Cautions

I hope that everyone will very carefully and seriously read, study, and digest what I have to say on these matters.

It is imperative that all persons should travel both ways by their own train. Changing to other trains, and particularly staying for later trains, cannot be allowed, as such irregularities upset the arrangements, and seriously interfere with the comfort of the proper occupants of such Trains. All persons detected breaking this urgent regulation will be left behind at Burton or Yarmouth as the case may be, and the Excursion Ticket will be forfeited. By the number on the ticket I can tell conclusively to what Department and Train the holder belongs. It must be distinctly understood that I will not undertake to provide room in other Trains for persons who deliberately disregard this most important instruction. To say the least of it, those persons who deliberately miss the earlier trains coming home are most inconsiderate of other people's comfort, and I hope this is the last time that I shall have to refer to this annoying disregard of the arrangements. The Great Eastern Railway Company are most particular about you travelling by your own Train, and there will be trouble in store for any persons who do not do so. All tickets must be shown at the gates leading to the platforms at Yarmouth.

BASS'S TRIP TO YARMOUTH, BURTON ON TRENT

Wait until your train stops and is at rest at the Platform before attempting to enter your Compartment. It is most dangerous to enter moving Trains, and, to prevent accidents, I beg of all persons to avoid doing so both at Burton and at Yarmouth.

Read this warning:

Last night an excursion train was preparing to leave Warrenpoint for Dublin, when a young lady named Agnes Brady was killed. The carriages were being shunted, and so great was the rush for seats that Miss Brady was accidentally pushed off the platform. She fell between the carriages and was decapitated.

And this, from one of the crippled children under the care of Mr Groom:

When I was nearly four years old, my dear mother was taking me by rail to a distant town to see my father, who had gone there to work; mother was carrying my baby sister, and before the train quite stopped I tried to get into it, and in doing so fell between the platform and the train on to the rails. The carriage wheels of the train went over me, and cut off my left arm quite close to the shoulder and crushed the fingers of my right hand. They took me to the hospital, where I had to stay for eighteen months. The kind doctors and nurses saved part of my right hand, so that I am able to do many things for myself.

Do not crowd into the centre, end, or front of the trains –

distribute yourselves regularly along the platform so that when the train draws up you can get a compartment without difficulty. The compartments in the front of all the trains must be fully occupied both morning and night.

Read the following warning:

Attention is drawn to the extremely dangerous practice on the part of passengers of opening carriage doors whilst the train is steaming into the station by the fact that a railway porter at Dolgelly Station has been terribly injured as the result of such carelessness.

If it only led to the thoughtless passenger hurting himself it wouldn't so much matter, but as the safety of others is involved it ought to be put down with a large, firm foot.

Do not put your head out of the carriage windows, or allow children especially to do so, as it is highly dangerous, owing to bridges, tunnels, signal posts, &c.

If any corridor carriages are used, be very careful that the outer doors in the corridor are not opened whilst the train is in motion. Many accidents have been recently caused by such carelessness.

There seems to be an impression that a family, of say 5 or 6 persons has a right to the whole of the compartment to the exclusion of other passengers – this cannot be allowed – all Third Class compartments must have 8 persons seated, and, if necessary, 9 or 10 – the same as in ordinary trains – the seating

STATION STREET, BURTON ON TRENT

is arranged for 5 on each side, except that lavatory compartments seat only 9 persons.

See that the doors of your compartment are securely fastened before the train starts – both morning and night – and do not attempt to open them again, or allow any of the occupants of your compartment to do so, until the train is at rest at the platform.

In case of sudden illness, or other urgent cause for stopping the train, pull down the communication chain which will be found above the windows in your compartment, and the officials will then stop the train at once.

It may interest passengers who are mischievously inclined, and who sometimes feel tempted to pull the communication chain to see what would happen, to know that the chain, after being pulled, hangs loosely in the compartment, and cannot be got back to its former position except by turning the red discs. The guard is therefore able to quickly discover in which compartment the mischief was done.

The penalty for the improper use of this alarm signal is £5.

Notwithstanding all my warnings, I regret to say that, on the return journey from Liverpool last year, a small lemonade bottle was thrown from No. 14 train, going right through the signal box window at St Michael's Station. Fortunately the signalman was at the other end of his box, and so escaped injury. Such a thoughtless act should haunt the culprit for ever, as the signalman might easily have been killed on the spot.

In a recent circular the management of various railways ask that it be made a matter of conscience for all passengers to place restraint upon travellers in the same compartment who may be tempted to commit this offence. Empty bottles, paper, &c., should be left in the racks, or under the seats of the carriages.

Passengers are requested not to put their feet on the cushions of seats of the carriages, but to protect the property of the Railway Companies, and especially to see that no windows are broken. Wilful damage must be paid for.

Do not throw away lighted matches, &c. – It is a most dangerous practice, and frequently I have seen ladies' dresses ruined through taking fire, to say nothing of the great risk to life. I need scarcely tell you – the married men anyway – that, in the summer, ladies' dresses are made of very light materials and so very easily take fire. Be careful, therefore, to put out all lighted matches, &c., before throwing them down on the floors of the carriages, on the platforms, on the piers, on the steamers, at the places of entertainment, or in the streets.

Do not throw orange peel or banana skins on the platforms or pavements. – It is very dangerous to passers-by, and serious accidents have happened to persons treading on such things and slipping down. The vexed question as to which is the more malignant the banana skin or orange peel, has been decided once and for all. A London daily states that 'the orange peel fall is not to be compared with the long slithering slide, ending in a violent collapse, which awaits the person unfortunate enough to step on a banana skin.' One railway company has recently prohibited the sale of oranges and bananas at their stations, owing to the danger arising from the peel and the skins being carelessly thrown down on the platforms by purchasers.

BURTON FAMILY

Baskets are usually to be found at convenient places for the reception of such things, waste paper, &c., which will prevent accidents, and keep the thoroughfares, &c., clean and tidy. These should be used in future.

May I specially beg of all persons to be quiet and orderly on the journeys, on the steamers, at the various places of amusement, in the streets, and generally throughout the day? It should be remembered that we have visited Yarmouth on four previous occasions; let it, therefore, be again said that all Bass & Co.'s Employees knew how to behave themselves, and that all returned home perfectly orderly and sober.

The Yarmouth people will, I am assured, again give us a hearty welcome, let nothing therefore occur throughout the day to disturb the harmony of our visit.

Upon the arrival of the last train at Yarmouth, I shall send a telegram to Messrs Bass & Co. announcing the same, which will be exhibited to their Old Brewery Yard Gates, in High Street – a similar telegram will also be sent to Mr J.M. Jacques, at the Midland Railway Station, Burton. The information contained in these messages will be for the friends of the excursionists, and may be relied upon as being true. These telegrams should reach Burton about 11.30, if the trains are running to time. The friends of the excursionists are therefore advised to take no notice whatever of absurd rumours of

accidents, &c. (often circulated by unthinking people), but to wait for my messages, which will be sent from Yarmouth as early as possible after the arrival of the last train.

*Extracts from Bass's staff trip book 1909*

## HIS WORSHIP THE GOOSEDRIVER

It was an amiable but deceitful afternoon in the third week of December. Snow fell heavily in the windows of confectioners' shops, and Father Christmas smiled in Keats's Bazaar the fawning smile of a myth who knows himself to be exploded; but beyond these and similar efforts to remedy the forgetfulness of a careless climate, there was no sign anywhere in the Five Towns, and especially in Bursley, of the immediate approach of the season of peace, goodwill, and gluttony on earth.

At the Tiger, next door to Keats's in the market-place, Mr Josiah Topham Curtenty had put down his glass (the port was kept specially for him), and told his boon companion, Mr Gordon, that he must be going. These two men had one powerful sentiment in common: they loved the same woman. Mr Curtenty, aged twenty-six in heart, thirty-six in mind, and

DARLASTON COUNCILLORS

WEDGWOOD INSTITUTE, BURSLEM

forty-six in looks, was fifty-six only in years. He was a rich man; he had made money as an earthenware manufacturer in the good old times before Satan was ingenious enough to invent German competition, American tariffs, and the price of coal; he was still making money with the aid of his son Harry, who now managed the works, but he never admitted that he was making it. No one has yet succeeded, and no one ever will succeed, in catching an earthenware manufacturer in the act of making money; he may confess with a sigh that he has performed the feat in the past, he may give utterance to a vague, preposterous hope that he will perform it again in the remote future, but as for surprising him in the very act, you would as easily surprise a hen laying an egg. Nowadays Mr Curtenty, commercially secure, spent most of his energy in helping to shape and control the high destinies of the town. He was Deputy-Mayor, and Chairman of the General Purposes Committee of the Town Council; he was also a Guardian of the Poor, a Justice of the Peace, President of the Society for the Prosecution of Felons, a sidesman, an Oddfellow, and several other things that meant dining, shrewdness, and good-nature. He was a short, stiff, stout, red-faced man, jolly with the jollity that springs from a kind heart, a humorous disposition, a perfect digestion, and the respectful

deference of one's bank-manager. Without being a member of the Browning Society, he held firmly to the belief that all's right with the world.

Mr Gordon, who was but a sorry part in the drama, was a younger, quieter, less forceful person, rather shy; a municipal mediocrity, perhaps a little inflated that day by reason of his having been elected to the Chairmanship of the Gas and Lighting Committee.

Both men had sat on their committee at the Town Hall across the way that deceitful afternoon, and we see them now, after refreshment well earned and consumed, about to separate and sink into private life. But as they came out into the portico of the Tiger, the famous Calypso-like barmaid of the Tiger a hovering enchantment in the background, it occurred that a flock of geese were meditating, as geese will, in the middle of the road. The gooseherd, a shabby middle-aged man, looked as though he had recently lost the Battle of Marathon, and was asking himself whether the path of his retreat might not lie through the bar-parlour of the Tiger.

'Business pretty good?' Mr Curtenty inquired of him cheerfully.

In the Five Towns business takes the place of weather as a topic of salutation.

65

TUNSTALL

'Business!' echoed the gooseherd.

In that one unassisted noun, scorning the aid of verb, adjective, or adverb, the gooseherd, by a masterpiece of profound and subtle emphasis, contrived to express the fact that he existed in a world of dead illusions, that he had become a convert to Schopenhauer, and that Mr Curtenty's inapposite geniality was a final grievance to him.

'There ain't no business!' he added.

'Ah!' returned Mr Curtenty, thoughtful: such an assertion of the entire absence of business was a reflection upon the town.

'Sithee!' said the gooseherd in ruthless accents, 'I druv these 'ere geese into this 'ere town this morning.' (Here he exaggerated the number of miles traversed.) 'Twelve geese and two gander – a Brent and a Barnacle. And how many is there now? How many?'

'Fourteen,' said Mr Gordon, having counted; and Mr. Curtenty gazed at him in reproach, for that he, a Town Councillor, had thus mathematically demonstrated the commercial decadence of Bursley.

'Market overstocked, eh?' Mr Curtenty suggested, throwing a side-glance at Callear the poulterer's close by, which was crammed with everything that flew, swam, or waddled.

'Call this a market?' said the gooseherd. 'I'st tak' my lot over to Hanbridge, wheer there *is* a bit doing, by all accounts.'

Now, Mr Curtenty had not the least intention of buying those geese, but nothing could be better calculated to straighten the back of a Bursley man than a reference to the mercantile activity of Hanbridge, that Chicago of the Five Towns.

'How much for the lot?' he inquired.

In that moment he reflected upon his reputation; he knew that he was a cure, a card, a character; he knew that everyone would think it just like Jos Curtenty, the renowned Deputy-Mayor of Bursley, to stand on the steps of the Tiger and pretend to chaffer with a gooseherd for a flock of geese. His imagination caught the sound of an oft-repeated inquiry, 'Did ye hear about old Jos's latest – trying to buy them there geese?' and the appreciative laughter that would follow.

The gooseherd faced him in silence.

'Well,' said Mr Curtenty again, his eyes twinkling, 'how much for the lot?'

The gooseherd gloomily and suspiciously named a sum.

Mr Curtenty named a sum startlingly less, ending in sixpence.

'I'll tak' it,' said the gooseherd, in a tone that closed on the bargain like a vice.

The Deputy-Mayor perceived himself the owner of twelve geese and two ganders – one Brent, one Barnacle. It was a shock, but he sustained it. Involuntarily he looked at Mr Gordon.

'How are you going to get 'em home, Curtenty?' asked Gordon, with coarse sarcasm; 'drive 'em?'

Nettled, Mr Curtenty retorted:

'Now, then, Gas Gordon!'

FUNERAL PROCESSION, BURSLEM

The barmaid laughed aloud at this sobriquet, which that same evening was all over the town, and which has stuck ever since to the Chairman of the Gas and Lighting Committee. Mr Gordon wished, and has never ceased to wish, either that he had been elected to some other committee, or that his name had begun with some other letter.

The gooseherd received the purchase-money like an affront, but when Mr Curtenty, full of private mirth, said, 'Chuck us your stick in,' he gave him the stick, and smiled under reservation. Jos Curtenty had no use for the geese; he could conceive no purpose which they might be made to serve, no smallest corner for them in his universe. Nevertheless, since he had rashly stumbled into a ditch, he determined to emerge from it grandly, impressively, magnificently. He instantaneously formed a plan by which he would snatch victory out of defeat. He would take Gordon's suggestion, and himself drive the geese up to his residence in Hillport, that lofty and aristocratic suburb. It would be an immense, an unparalleled farce; a wonder, a topic for years, the crown of his reputation as a card.

He announced his intention with that misleading sobriety and ordinariness of tone which it has been the foible of many great humorists to assume. Mr Gordon lifted his head several times very quickly, as if to say, 'What next?' and then actually departed, which was a clear proof that the man had no imagination and no soul.

The gooseherd winked.

'You be rightly called "Curtenty", mester,' said he, and passed into the Tiger.

BURSLEM

OSWIN A. WILLCOX
GROCER & BAKER
HANLEY

HANLEY

'That's the best joke I ever heard,' Jos said to himself. 'I wonder whether he saw it.'

Then the procession of the geese and the Deputy-Mayor commenced. Now, it is not to be assumed that Mr Curtenty was necessarily bound to look foolish in the driving of geese. He was no nincompoop. On the contrary, he was one of those men who, bringing common-sense and presence of mind to every action of their lives, do nothing badly, and always escape the ridiculous. He marshalled his geese with notable gumption, adopted towards them exactly the correct stress of persuasion, and presently he smiled to see them preceding him in the direction of Hillport. He looked neither to right nor left, but simply at his geese, and thus the quidnuncs of the market-place and the supporters of shop-fronts were unable to catch his eye. He tried to feel like a gooseherd; and such was his histrionic quality, his instinct for the dramatic, he *was* a gooseherd, despite his blue Melton overcoat, his hard felt hat with the flattened top, and that opulent-curving collar which was the secret despair of the young dandies of Hillport. He had the most natural air in the world. The geese were the victims of this imaginative effort of Mr Curtenty's. They took him seriously as a gooseherd. These fourteen intelligences, each with an object in life, each bent on self-aggrandizement and the satisfaction of desires, began to follow the line of least

resistance in regard to the superior intelligence unseen but felt behind them, feigning, as geese will, that it suited them so to submit, and that in reality they were still quite independent. But in the peculiar eye of the Barnacle gander, who was leading, an observer with sufficient fancy might have deciphered a mild revolt against this triumph of the absurd, the accidental, and the futile; a passive yet Promethean spiritual defiance of the supreme powers.

Mr Curtenty got his fourteen intelligences safely across the top of St Luke's Square, and gently urged them into the steep defile of Oldcastle Street. By this time rumour had passed in front of him and run off down side-streets like water let into an irrigation system. At every corner was a knot of people, at most windows a face. And the Deputy-Mayor never spoke nor smiled. The farce was enormous; the memory of it would survive revolutions and religions.

Halfway down Oldcastle Street the first disaster happened. Electric tramways had not then knitted the Five Towns in a network of steel; but the last word of civilization and refinement was about to be uttered, and a gang of men were making patterns with wires on the skyscape of Oldcastle Street. One of the wires, slipping from its temporary gripper, swirled with an extraordinary sound into the roadway, and writhed there in spirals. Several of Mr Curtenty's geese were

68

HOSPITAL SATURDAY, UTTOXETER

knocked down, and rose obviously annoyed; but the Barnacle gander fell with a clinging circle of wire round his muscular, glossy neck, and did not rise again. It was a violent, mysterious, agonizing, and sudden death for him, and must have confirmed his theories about the arbitrariness of things. The thirteen passed pitilessly on. Mr Curtenty freed the gander from the coiling wire, and picked it up, but, finding it far too heavy to carry, he handed it to a Corporation road-sweeper.

'I'll send for it,' he said; 'wait here.'

These were the only words uttered by him during a memorable journey.

The second disaster was that the deceitful afternoon turned to rain – cold, cruel rain, persistent rain, full of sinister significance. Mr Curtenty ruefully raised the velvet of his Melton. As he did so a brougham rolled into Oldcastle Street, a little in front of him, from the directions of St Peter's Church, and vanished towards Hillport. He knew the carriage; he had bought it and paid for it. Deep, far down, in his mind stirred the thought:

'I'm just the least bit glad she didn't see me.'

He had the suspicion, which recurs even to optimists, that happiness is after all a chimera.

The third disaster was that the sun set and darkness descended. Mr Curtenty had, unfortunately, not reckoned with this diurnal phenomenon; he had not thought upon the undesirability of being under compulsion to drive geese by the sole illumination of gas-lamps lighted by Corporation gas.

THE ADMIRAL JERVIS, OAKAMOOR

MARKET DAY, UTTOXETER

ROLLESTON

After this disasters multiplied. Dark and the rain had transformed the farce into something else. It was five-thirty when at last he reached The Firs, and the garden of The Firs was filled with lamentable complainings of a remnant of geese. His man Pond met him with a stable-lantern.

'Damp, sir,' said Pond.

'Oh, nowt to speak of,' said Mr Curtenty, and, taking off his hat, he shot the fluid contents of the brim into Pond's face. It was his way of dotting the 'i' of irony. 'Missis come in?'

'Yes, sir; I have but just rubbed the horse down.'

So far no reference to the surrounding geese, all forlorn in the heavy winter rain.

'I've gotten two or three geese and one gander here for Christmas,' said Mr Curtenty after a pause. To inferiors he always used the dialect.

'Yes, sir.'

'Turn 'em into th' orchard, as you call it.'

'Yes, sir.'

'They aren't all there. Thou mun put th' horse in the trap and fetch the rest thysen.'

'Yes, sir.'

'One's dead. A roadman's takkin' care on it in Oldcastle Street. He'll wait for thee. Give him sixpence.'

'Yes, sir.'

'There's another got into th' cut [canal].'

'Yes, sir.'

'There's another strayed on the railway-line – happen it's run over by this.'

70

'Yes, sir.'

'And one's making the best of her way to Oldcastle. I couldna coax her in here.'

'Yes, sir.'

'Collect 'em.'

'Yes, sir.'

Mr Curtenty walked away towards the house.

'Mester!' Pond called after him, flashing the lantern.

'Well, lad?'

'There's no gander i' this lot.'

'Hast forgotten to count thysen?' Mr Curtenty answered blithely from the shelter of the side-door.

But within himself he was a little crestfallen to think that the surviving gander should have escaped his vigilance, even in the darkness. He had set out to drive the geese home, and he had driven them home, most of them. He had kept his temper, his dignity, his cheerfulness. He had got a bargain in geese. So much was indisputable ground for satisfaction. And yet the feeling of an anticlimax would not be dismissed. Upon the whole, his transit lacked glory. It had begun in splendour, but it had ended in discomfort and almost ignominy. Nevertheless, Mr Curtenty's unconquerable soul asserted itself in a quite genuine and tuneful whistle as he entered the house.

The fate of the Brent gander was never ascertained.

The dining-room of The Firs was a spacious and inviting refectory, which owed nothing of its charm to William Morris, Regent Street, or the Arts and Crafts Society. Its triple aim was richness, solidity, and comfort, but especially comfort; and this aim was achieved in new oak furniture of immovable firmness, in a Turkey carpet which swallowed up the feet like a feather bed, and in large oil-paintings, whose darkly-glinting frames were a guarantee of their excellence. On a winter's night, as now, the room was at its richest, solidest, most comfortable. The blue plush curtains were drawn on their stout brass rods across the door and French window. Finest selected silkstone fizzed and flamed in a patent grate which had the extraordinary gift of radiating heat into the apartment instead of the chimney. The shaded Welsbach lights of the chandelier cast a dazzling luminance on the tea-table of snow and silver, while leaving the pictures in a gloom so discreet that not Ruskin himself could have decided whether these were by Whistler or Peter Paul Rubens. On either side of the marble mantelpiece were two easy-chairs of an immense, incredible capacity, chairs of crimson plush for Titans, chairs softer than moss, more pliant than a loving heart, more enveloping than a caress. In one of these chairs, that to the left of the fireplace, Mr Curtenty was accustomed to snore every Saturday and Sunday afternoon, and almost every evening. The other was usually empty, but tonight it was occupied by Mrs Curtenty, the jewel of the casket. In the presence of her

KINGSWINFORD

husband she always used a small rocking-chair of ebonized cane.

To glance at this short, slight, yet plump little creature as she reclined crosswise in the vast chair, leaving great spaces of the seat unfilled, was to think rapturously to one's self: *This is a woman.* Her fluffy head was such a dot against the back of the chair, the curve of her chubby ringed hand above the head was so adorable, her black eyes were so provocative, her slippered feet so wee – yes, and there was something so mysteriously thrilling about the fall of her skirt that you knew instantly her name was Clara, her temper both fiery and obstinate, and her personality distracting. You knew that she was one of those women of frail physique who can endure fatigues that would destroy a camel; one of those demonic women capable of doing without sleep for ten nights in order to nurse you; capable of dying and seeing you die rather than give way about the tint of a necktie; capable of laughter and tears simultaneously; capable of never being in the wrong except for the idle whim of so being. She had a big mouth and very wide nostrils, and her years were thirty-five. It was no matter; it would have been no matter had she been a hundred and thirty-five. In short . . .

Clara Curtenty wore tight-fitting black silk, with a long gold chain that descended from her neck nearly to her waist, and was looped up in the middle to an old-fashioned gold brooch. She was in mourning for a distant relative. Black pre-eminently suited her. Consequently her distant relatives died at frequent intervals.

The basalt clock on the mantelpiece trembled and burst into the song of six. Clara Curtenty rose swiftly from the easy-chair, and took her seat in front of the tea-tray. Almost at the same moment a neat black-and-white parlour-maid brought in teapot, copper kettle, and a silver-covered dish containing hot pikelets; then departed. Clara was alone again; not the same Clara now, but a personage demure, prim, precise, frightfully upright of back – a sort of impregnable stronghold – without doubt a Deputy Mayoress.

At five past six Josiah Curtenty entered the room, radiant from a hot bath, and happy in dry clothes – a fine, if mature, figure of a man. His presence filled the whole room.

'Well, my chuck!' he said, and kissed her on the cheek.

She gazed at him with a look that might mean anything. Did she raise her cheek to his greeting, or was it fancy that she had endured, rather than accepted, his kiss? He was scarcely sure. And if she had endured instead of accepting the kiss, was her mood to be attributed to his lateness for tea, or to the fact that she was aware of the episode of the geese? He could not divine.

'Pikelets! Good!' he exclaimed, taking the cover off the dish.

This strong, successful, and dominant man adored his wife, and went in fear of her. She was his first love, but his second spouse. They had been married ten years. In those ten years they had quarrelled only five times, and she had changed the very colour of his life. Till his second marriage he had boasted that he belonged to the people and retained the habits of the people. Clara, though she also belonged to the people, very soon altered all that. Clara had a passion for the genteel. Like

MULBERRY HOUSE, HANLEY

many warm-hearted, honest, clever, and otherwise sensible persons, Clara was a snob, but a charming little snob. She ordered him to forget that he belonged to the people. She refused to listen when he talked in the dialect. She made him dress with opulence, and even with tidiness; she made him buy a fashionable house and fill it with fine furniture; she made him buy a brougham in which her gentility could pay calls and do shopping (she shopped at Oldcastle, where a decrepit aristocracy of tradesmen sneered at Hanbridge's lack of style); she had her 'day'; she taught the servants to enter the reception-rooms without knocking; she took tea in bed in the morning, and tea in the afternoon in the drawing-room. She would have instituted dinner at seven, but she was a wise woman, and realized that too much tyranny often means revolution and the crumbling of thrones; therefore the ancient plebeian custom of high tea at six was allowed to persist and continue.

She it was who had compelled Josiah (or bewitched, beguiled, coaxed and wheedled him), after a public refusal, to accept the unusual post of Deputy-Mayor. In two years' time he might count on being Mayor. Why, then, should Clara have been so anxious for this secondary dignity? Because, in that year of royal festival, Bursley, in common with many other boroughs, had had a fancy to choose a Mayor out of the House of Lords. The Earl of Chell, a magnate of the county, had consented to wear the mayoral chain and dispense the mayoral hospitalities on condition that he was provided with a deputy for daily use.

It was the idea of herself being deputy to the lovely, meddlesome, and arrogant Countess of Chell that had appealed to Clara.

The deputy of a Countess at length spoke.

'Will Harry be late at the works again tonight?' she asked in her colder, small-talk manner, which committed her to nothing, as Josiah well knew.

Her way of saying that word 'Harry' was inimitably significant. She gave it an air. She liked Harry, and she liked Harry's name, because it had a Kensingtonian sound. Harry, so accomplished in business, was also a dandy, and he was a dog. 'My stepson' — she loved to introduce him, so tall, manly, distinguished, and dandiacal. Harry, enriched by his own mother, belonged to a London club; he ran down to Llandudno for week-ends; and it was reported that he had been behind the scenes at the Alhambra. Clara felt for the word 'Harry' the unreasoning affection which most women lavish on 'George'.

'Like as not,' said Josiah. 'I haven't been to the works this afternoon.'

Another silence fell, and then Josiah, feeling himself unable to bear any further suspense as to his wife's real mood and temper, suddenly determined to tell her all about the geese, and know the worst. And precisely at the instant that he

SNOW HILL, SHELTON

opened his mouth, the maid opened the door and announced:

'Mr Duncalf wishes to see you at once, sir. He won't keep you a minute.'

'Ask him in here, Mary,' said the Deputy-Mayoress sweetly; 'and bring another cup and saucer.'

Mr Duncalf was the Town Clerk of Bursley: legal, portly, dry, and a little shy.

'I won't stop, Curtenty. How d'ye do, Mrs Curtenty? No, thanks, really —' But she, smiling, exquisitely gracious, flattered and smoothed him into a chair.

'Any interesting news, Mr Duncalf?' she said, and added: 'But we're glad that *anything* should have brought you in.'

'Well,' said Mr Duncalf, 'I've just had a letter by the afternoon post from Lord Chell.'

'Oh, the Earl! Indeed; how very interesting.'

'What's he after?' inquired Josiah cautiously.

'He says he's just been appointed Governor of East Australia – announcement'll be in tomorrow's papers – and so he must regretfully resign the mayoralty. Says he'll pay the fine, but of course we shall have to remit that by special resolution of the Council.'

'Well, I'm dammed!' Josiah exclaimed.

'Topham!' Mrs Curtenty remonstrated, but with a delightful acquitting dimple. She never would call him Josiah, much less

Jos. Topham came more easily to her lips, and sometimes Top.

'Your husband,' said Mr Duncalf impressively to Clara, 'will, of course, have to step into the Mayor's shoes, and you'll have to fill the place of the Countess.' He paused, and added: 'And very well you'll do it, too – very well. Nobody better.'

The Town Clerk frankly admired Clara.

'Mr Duncalf – Mr Duncalf!' She raised a finger at him. 'You are the most shameless flatterer in the town.'

The flatterer was flattered. Having delivered the weighty news, he had leisure to savour his own importance as the bearer of it. He drank a cup of tea. Josiah was thoughtful, but Clara brimmed over with a fascinating loquacity. Then Mr Duncalf said that he must really be going, and, having arranged with the Mayor-elect to call a special meeting of the Council at once, he did go, all the while wishing he had the enterprise to stay.

Josiah accompanied him to the front-door. The sky had now cleared.

'Thank ye for calling,' said the host.

'Oh, that's all right. Good-night, Curtenty. Got that goose out of the canal?'

So the story was all abroad!

Josiah turned to the dining-room, imperceptibly smiling. At the door the sight of his wife halted him. The face of that

74

WHEELING OUT THE DRUNK, ROEBUCK INN, HANLEY

NORMACOT

precious and adorable woman flamed out lightning and all menace and offence. Her luring eyes showed what a triumph of dissimulation she must have achieved in the presence of Mr Duncalf, but now she could speak her mind.

'Yes, Topham!' she exploded, as though finishing an harangue. 'And on this day of all days you choose to drive geese in the public road behind my carriage!'

Jos was stupefied, annihilated.

'Did you see me, then, Clarry?'

He vainly tried to carry it off.

'Did I see you? Of course I saw you!'

She withered him up with the hot wind of scorn.

'Well,' he said foolishly, 'how was I to know that the Earl would resign just today?'

'How were you to — ?'

Harry came in for his tea. He glanced from one to the other, discreet, silent. On the way home he had heard the tale of the geese in seven different forms. The Deputy-Mayor, so soon to be Mayor, walked out of the room.

'Pond has just come back, father,' said Harry; 'I drove up the hill with him.'

And as Josiah hesitated a moment in the hall, he heard Clara exclaim, 'Oh, Harry!'

'Damn!' he murmured.

The *Signal* of the following day contained the announcement which Mr Duncalf had forecast; it also stated, on authority, that Mr Josiah Curtenty would wear the mayoral chain of Bursley immediately, and added as its own private opinion that, in default of the Right Honourable the Earl of Chell and his Countess, no better 'civic heads' could have been found than Mr Curtenty and his charming wife. So far the tone of the *Signal* was unimpeachable. But underneath all this was a sub-title, 'Amusing Exploit of the Mayor-elect', followed by an amusing description of the procession of the geese, a description which concluded by referring to Mr Curtenty as His Worship the Goosedriver.

Hanbridge, Knype, Longshaw, and Turnhill laughed heartily, and perhaps a little viciously, at this paragraph, but Bursley was annoyed by it. In print the affair did not look at all well. Bursley prided itself on possessing a unique dignity as the 'Mother of the Five Towns', and to be presided over by a goosedriver, however humorous and hospitable he might be, did not consort with that dignity. A certain Mayor of Longshaw, years before, had driven a sow to market, and derived a tremendous advertisement therefrom, but Bursley had no wish to rival Longshaw in any particular. Bursley

THE FOAMING QUART, BURSLEM

regarded Longshaw as the Inferno of the Five Towns. In Bursley you were bidden to go to Longshaw as you were bidden to go to . . . Certain acute people in Hillport saw nothing but a paralysing insult in the opinion of the *Signal* (first and foremost a Hanbridge organ), that Bursley could find no better civic head than Josiah Curtenty. At least three Aldermen and seven Councillors privately, and in the Tiger, disagreed with any such view of Bursley's capacity to find heads.

And underneath all this brooding dissatisfaction lurked the thought, as the alligator lurks in a muddy river, that 'the Earl wouldn't like it' – meaning the geese episode. It was generally felt that the Earl had been badly treated by Jos Curtenty. The town could not explain its sentiments – could not argue about them. They were not, in fact, capable of logical justification; but they were there, they violently existed. It would have been useless to point out that if the inimitable Jos had not been called to the mayoralty the episode of the geese would have passed as a gorgeous joke; that everyone had been vastly amused by it until that desolating issue of the *Signal* announced the Earl's retirement; that Jos Curtenty could not possibly have foreseen what was about to happen; and that, anyhow, goose-driving was less a crime than a social solecism,

and less a social solecism than a brilliant eccentricity. Bursley was hurt, and logic is no balm for wounds.

Some may ask: If Bursley was offended, why did it not mark its sense of Josiah's failure to read the future by electing another Mayor? The answer is, that while all were agreed that his antic was inexcusable, all were equally agreed to pretend that it was a mere trifle of no importance; you cannot deprive a man of his prescriptive right for a mere trifle of no importance. Besides, nobody could be so foolish as to imagine that goosedriving, though reprehensible in a Mayor about to succeed an Earl, is an act of which official notice can be taken.

The most curious thing in the whole imbroglio is that Josiah Curtenty secretly agreed with his wife and the town. He was ashamed, overset. His procession of geese appeared to him in an entirely new light, and he had the strength of mind to admit to himself, 'I've made a fool of myself.'

Harry went to London for a week, and Josiah, under plea of his son's absence, spent eight hours a day at the works. The brougham remained in the coach-house.

The Town Council duly met in special conclave, and Josiah Topham Curtenty became Mayor of Bursley.

Shortly after Christmas it was announced that the Mayor and Mayoress had decided to give a New Year's treat to four

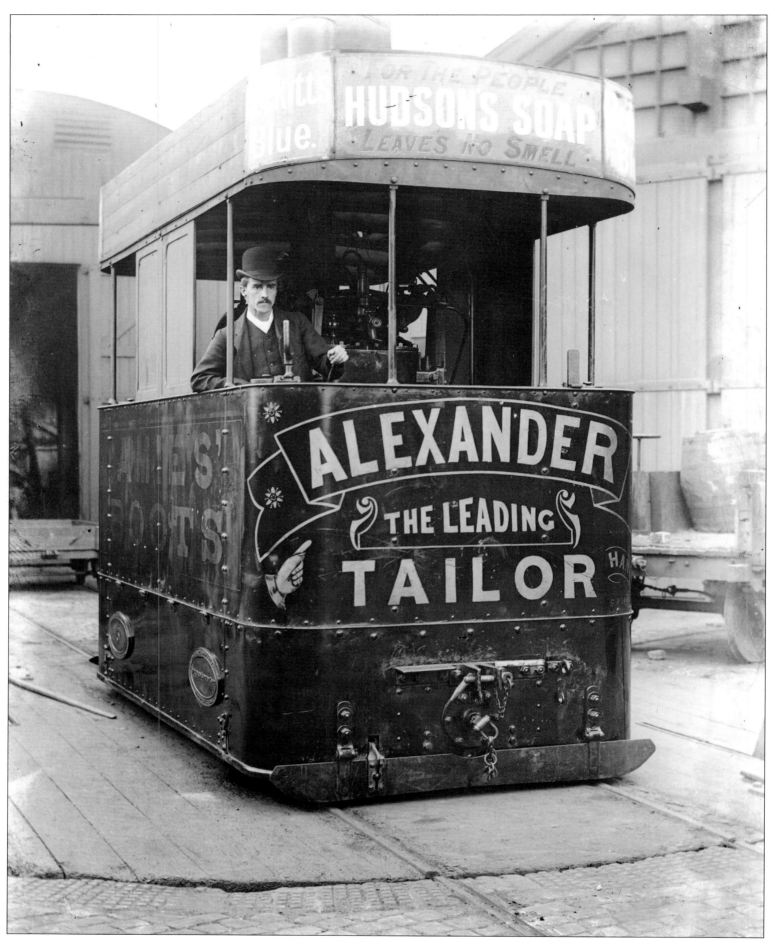

STEAM TRAM, STOKE

COTTAGE HOMES SCHOOL, WOLVERHAMPTON

hundred poor old people in the St Luke's covered market. It was also spread about that this treat would eclipse and extinguish all previous treats of a similar nature, and that it might be accepted as some slight foretaste of the hospitality which the Mayor and Mayoress would dispense in that memorable year of royal festival. The treat was to occur on January 9, the Mayoress's birthday.

On January 7 Josiah happened to go home early. He was proceeding into the drawing-room without enthusiasm to greet his wife, when he heard voices within; and one voice was the voice of Gas Gordon.

Jos stood still. It has been mentioned that Gordon and the Mayor were in love with the same woman. The Mayor had easily captured her under the very guns of his not formidable rival, and he had always thereafter felt a kind of benevolent, good-humoured, contemptuous pity for Gordon – Gordon, whose life was a tragic blank; Gordon, who lived, a melancholy and defeated bachelor, with his mother and two unmarried sisters older than himself. That Gordon still worshipped at the shrine did not disturb him; on the contrary, it pleased him. Poor Gordon!

'But, really, Mrs Curtenty,' Gordon was saying – 'really, you know I – that – is – really —'

'To please me!' Mrs Curtenty entreated, with a seductive charm that Jos felt even outside the door.

Then there was a pause.

'Very well,' said Gordon.

Mr Curtenty tiptoed away and back into the street. He walked in the dark nearly to Oldcastle, and returned about six o'clock. But Clara said no word of Gordon's visit. She had scarcely spoken to Topham for three weeks.

The next morning, as Harry was departing to the works, Mrs Curtenty followed the handsome youth into the hall.

'Harry,' she whispered, 'bring me two ten-pound notes this afternoon, will you, and say nothing to your father.'

Gas Gordon was to be on the platform at the poor people's treat. As he walked down Trafalgar Road his eye caught a still-exposed fragment of a decayed bill on a boarding. It referred to a meeting of the local branch of the Anti-Gambling League a year ago in the lecture-hall of the Wesleyan Chapel, and it said that Councillor Gordon would occupy the chair on that occasion. Mechanically Councillor Gordon stopped and tore the fragment away from the boarding.

The treat, which took the form of a dinner, was an unqualified success; it surpassed all expectations. Even the diners themselves were satisfied – a rare thing at such affairs.

A STAFFORDSHIRE GIG

Goose was a prominent item in the menu. After the repast the replete guests were entertained from the platform, the Mayor being, of course, in the chair. Harry sang 'In Old Madrid', accompanied by his stepmother, with faultless expression. Mr Duncalf astonished everybody with the famous North-Country recitation, 'The Patent Hair-brushing Mashane'. There were also a banjo solo, a skirt dance of discretion, and a campanological turn. At last, towards ten o'clock, Mr Gordon, who had hitherto done nothing, rose in his place, amid good-natured cries of 'Gas!'

'I feel sure you will all agree with me,' he began, 'that this evening would not be complete without a vote of thanks – a very hearty vote of thanks – to our excellent host and chairman.'

Ear-splitting applause.

'I've got a little story to tell you,' he continued – 'a story that up to this moment has been a close secret between his Worship the Mayor and myself.' His Worship looked up sharply at the speaker. 'You've heard about some geese, I reckon. (*Laughter.*) Well, you've not heard all, but I'm going to tell you. I can't keep it to myself any longer. You think his Worship drove those geese – I hope they're digesting well (*loud laughter*) – just for fun. He didn't. I was with him when he bought them, and I happened to say that goosedriving was a very difficult accomplishment.'

'Depends on the geese!' shouted a voice.

'Yes, it does,' Mr. Gordon admitted. 'Well, his Worship contradicted me, and we had a bit of an argument. I don't bet, as you know – at least, not often – but I don't mind confessing that I offered to bet him a sovereign he couldn't drive his geese half a mile. "Look here, Gordon," he said to me: "there's a lot of distress in the town just now – trade bad, and so on, and so on. I'll lay you a level ten pounds I drive these geese to Hillport myself, the loser to give the money to charity." "Done," I said. "Don't say anything about it," he says. "I won't," I says – but I am doing. (*Applause.*) I feel it my duty to say something about it. (*More applause.*) Well, I lost, as you all know. He drove 'em to Hillport. ('*Good old Jos!*') That's not all. The Mayor insisted on putting his own ten pounds to mine and making it twenty. Here are the two identical notes, his and mine.' Mr Gordon waved the identical notes amid an uproar. 'We've decided that everyone who has dined here tonight shall receive a brand-new shilling. I see Mr Septimus Lovatt from the bank there with a bag. He will attend to you as you go out. (*Wild outbreak and tumult of rapturous applause.*) And now three cheers for your Mayor – and Mayoress!'

It was colossal, the enthusiasm.

'*And* for Gas Gordon!' called several voices.

The cheers rose again in surging waves.

Everyone remarked that the Mayor, usually so

80

UTTOXETER

imperturbable, was quite overcome – seemed as if he didn't know where to look.

Afterwards, as the occupants of the platform descended, Mr Gordon glanced into the eyes of Mrs Curtenty, and found there his exceeding reward. The mediocrity had blossomed out that evening into something new and strange. Liar, deliberate liar and self-accused gambler as he was, he felt that he had lived during that speech; he felt that it was the supreme moment of his life.

'What a perfectly wonderful man your husband is!' said Mrs Duncalf to Mrs Curtenty.

Clara turned to her husband with a sublime gesture of satisfaction. In the brougham, going home, she bewitched him with wifely endearments. She could afford to do so. The stigma of the geese episode was erased.

But the barmaid of the Tiger, as she let down her bright hair that night in the attic of the Tiger, said to herself, 'Well, of all the —' Just that.

*Arnold Bennett*

## FEMALE SCHOOL TEACHERS

Sir, – In your report of the meeting of the School Board, held last Friday, it will be noticed that the Board again discussed the question of female labour in boys' schools, and took another step in that direction by appointing another female assistant in a boys' school. The labour members have always strenuously opposed these appointments as being detrimental to the best interests of education, and crippling the prospects of male teachers by underselling them in the labour market.

Mr Corbett argues that female teachers are 'better qualified' than male teachers for the lower standards. It is remarkable that when the Board cannot get male teachers for the pittance they offer they suddenly discover that female teachers are easily obtained, and, what is stranger still, are 'better qualified' to undertake work hitherto discharged by male teachers. The labour members are bound by their principles to oppose this innovation, and have discharged their duty faithfully.

Their efforts have been defeated by the dominant majority on the Board. I do not think it is sufficient for working men to regard the stand they are making for trade unionist

STAR BANK, OAKAMOOR

CHEADLE

principles with silent approval, I believe an expression of opinion would strengthen their hands considerably, and make it clear that they are only representing the opinions of all true unionists – Thanking you for insertion, I remain, yours,
    Trade Unionist.

*Express and Star February 9, 1893*

## PROPERTY SALE AT CHEADLE

The sale of the late Mr Samuel Turner's property was concluded on Thursday evening at the Wheat Sheaf Hotel, when there was a very good attendance. Three dwelling-houses and gardens in Black-lane realized £220, Mrs Eli Bowers being the purchaser. Two dwelling-houses, a shop, and a large room at the rear, in Bank-street, were sold to Mrs Dunkley at £385. Two cottages in Oak-street sold for £75 to Mr R.H. Shufflebotham. Ten dwelling-houses at the Rindle were purchased by Mr E. Carnwell for £310. Two cottages at Trimpos were sold for £148 to Mr S.A. Turner. Three dwelling-houses at Trimpos sold for £187 to Mr G. Wood. Mr J. Hulme conducted the auction, and Messrs Thacker, Cull, and Brett, solicitors, represented the vendors.

*Staffordshire Advertiser May 12, 1894*

LEATHER PREPARERS AT WINCER AND PLANT, WALSALL

## JEWELLERY ROBBERY IN HORSLEY-FIELDS

Almost on the stroke of Tuesday midnight residents in Horsley-fields, Wolverhampton, such of them as had not retired for the night, were startled by the sound of glass smashing, two distinct crashes following each other rapidly. People in the immediate vicinity of Bradshaw Street at once rushed out of their houses, whereupon two men who appeared to be busily engaged at the window of Messrs Duncan Smith and Co., pawnbrokers, made off at top speed, a third taking to his heels in another direction. Upon examination it was found that the large plate-glass window, 12ft by 10ft had been shivered to atoms, and further inquiries revealed the fact that the thieves, although disturbed in their well-studied 'plant', had managed to abstract almost a score of silver watches of the aggregate value of £30, besides other oddments, while a card of gold rings had been hurriedly dropped on the pavement. To reach their plunder the rascals had had to cut through a blind drawn down outside the window, so that in every probability the robbery had been planned in broad daylight, and by someone acquainted with the lay of the premises. Ten minutes before midnight two men were seen standing near the Star Inn by a Mrs Smith, living at 132, Horsley-fields, and shortly after closing her door she heard the smashing of glass. Going downstairs she saw three men against the pawnshop window, and heard another crash, other people were attracted by the noise, and the men then decamped. So far the police have no clue.

*Express and Star March 30, 1893*

## ONE HUNDRED MILE RACE

The 100 miles bicycle race in connection with the Stone Cycling Club came off on Whit-Monday, the competitors being Wm. Nickisson and Wm. Mellor, both of Stone. The start was made punctually at six a.m. from the top of High-street, in the presence of a large number of spectators. When the first stage, to Newcastle and back, had been completed, Nickisson led by 5½ minutes. At the end of the outward journey at Grosvenor Bridge, Chester, he had increased his lead to ten minutes. Between Chester and Nantwich on the return journey Nickisson was several times seized with cramp, delaying him so that Mellor was enabled to overtake him, passing through Nantwich with 20 minutes to the good. Nickisson had now practically given up the race, but being met by his pacemaker, J. Jones, who took him in hand and

HORSE COLLAR MAKERS, WALSALL

gave him some nutriment, he revived and made a fresh start, and eleven miles further on caught up Mellor, and the two competitors rode nearly together for four or five miles. Nickisson was, however, a little quicker in getting up the hills, and at the top of Hatton Reservoir bank he had obtained a lead of 30 yards. When Darlaston Inn was reached Nickisson had increased his lead to 150 yards, and although Mellor made a splendid spurt along the Newcastle-road, it was useless, and Nickisson got in the winner by 50 yards. The time was 9 hours 38 minutes. Nickisson is a total abstainer, and had Bovril and raw eggs in place of stimulants.

*Staffordshire Advertiser May 19, 1894*

## DRAKELOW HALL

The carriage arrived to take us to Drakelow. It was mid-day when we started, the weather being all that could be desired for our trip; indeed, since we commenced our tour we have rejoiced in weather the like of which we can never remember, and it is certain we shall none of us ever forget the summer of

1887. After crossing the beautiful bridge over the Trent, we came to the picturesque recreation gardens stretching along its banks, where the Burtonians promenade, frequently to the music of one of the finest bands in the Midland Counties, and then drove through the village of Stapenhill, which extends nearly a mile up the hill side. After this, we found ourselves in open country – on one side of the road the gay fields waved yellow with corn in the summer breezes, and, on the other, we saw fields and meadows broken up by hedges covered with trailing plants, and heavy with wild berries. Bees were hanging on every clover head, and feasting on the sweets of the honeysuckle in the hedges, butterflies of many colours flitted by, and gaudy dragon flies, ever and anon, glanced gold and silver in the noon beams. Presently, we entered the domain of Drakelow, and its extensive park came into view. It is well wooded, and the intermixture of trees and lawn, as seen from the avenue, with the deer trooping in silent herds across the green sward, was a sight full of pleasing variety. As our carriage drove to the grand entrance, we had time to note the picturesque situation of the splendid old mansion, with its gables, its turrets, and its ivy-covered walls planted in a spot where nature is prodigal of beauty. On one side of the

THE GREEN, STAPENHILL

mansion, lofty walls enclose extensive gardens; on the other, and before it, the park, which stretches to the right and left, is studded with clumps of over-shadowing trees, beneath which herds of deer were browsing, whilst their fawns were skipping about hither and thither in great animation.

The river Trent runs along not far from the west front, and the eminence on which the house is built slopes to the water's edge. Descending from the carriage, we entered the house, passing through a noble billiard room into a long and spacious corridor, and then sauntered through a suite of handsome sitting-rooms, whose walls were covered with pictures, and whose floors were filled with antique furniture, rare cabinets of china, and articles of *vertu*. At the end of these apartments, we came to the celebrated dining saloon, which looks on to beautiful pleasure grounds. It has an elegantly decorated arched roof with a deep and ornamental recess at one end lined with lattice work. The walls and ceiling were covered with landscape views painted by a celebrated artist; the floors are of polished oak, and the mantel-piece, which is constructed of spa, quartz, mica, and stalactite stones, is a marvel of handiwork, and a picture of glittering beauty when lighted up at night.

After we had sufficiently admired these apartments, the library, the smoking-rooms, etc., and were perfected in all their details of wainscot, carvings, and decorations, our guide invited us to ascend the staircase to inspect the sleeping

BASS'S WATER TOWER, BURTON ON TRENT

TETTENHALL

apartments. As we proceeded thither, along the noble corridors, we were struck with astonishment at the costly contents of the cabinets which lined the walls from floor to ceiling – some of which contained rare old china and vases of priceless worth.

On reaching the floor above, we proceeded, along wide passages, to the various chambers, all of which contain carved oak furniture many centuries old. The most notable suites are the 'bachelors' and 'guests', the former being furnished in the 17th century style, and possessing carved bedsteads, black with age, surmounted with heavy canopies, also wardrobes, cabinets and chairs to match; whilst the latter possesses a similar style of furnishing of the 18th century, somewhat lighter in appearance, and the carving more graceful and intricate.

We took a peep into many other rooms, and then passed on to those inhabited by the family, which are equally antique, except Mrs Gretton's rooms, which embrace the old and new style of furnishing, and possess many beautiful works of art, and pictures of the 19th century. Proceeding along, we came to the apartments over the billiard room, and here rested awhile. From the windows we looked out on to the deer park, planted with glorious old trees, each heaped up with rich foliage, giving both shade and shelter to the wayfarer.

Retracing our steps, by passages and corridors, which lead up and down in beautiful confusion, we returned to the staircase, and then, descending to the vestibule, entered a deliciously quaint apartment, overlooking the river, wherein we dined. This room has an alcove or recess at one side, divided off by oak panels, and the walls are covered with family portraits and old paintings.

From every point of view, outside and inside, the mansion house of Drakelow is a most delightful residence. It is one of those dreamy old places in which a student, or a peace-loving and retiring man would delight to spend his days; containing rooms which smell of lavender, lattice windows which admit the perfume of the honeysuckle and roses from the gardens below, recesses and nooks to hide in, and old fashioned furniture and curiosities sufficient to satisfy an antiquary. After dinner, three of us wandered through the grounds to the rosary, and to the Dutch and Italian gardens; we were delighted with the general picturesque appearance and the taste displayed in their arrangement, for they are not only eminently striking, but correspond with the antiquity of the mansion. The pleasant partemes are divided by walks into a number of beds, where all kinds of beautiful flowers are to be seen; and, in the centre of the whole, underneath a canopy of

CYCLE CLUB, BURTON ON TRENT

FLOWER SHOW, BURTON ON TRENT

SALT MAKING, STAFFORD

PACKING SALT, STAFFORD

creepers, there is a splendid fountain.

Adjacent, there are lovers' gardens and lovers' walks, laid out ages ago by some poetic soul – places purposely made wherein to whisper tales of love, and to lose your heart. Or, if you are in a romantic or meditative mood, these sequestered avenues will tempt you to linger and dream to your heart's content.

*Alfred Barnard*

## LIFE OF A MALTSTER

When I went to Burton-on-Trent I asked a retired maltster about the malting process: 'Go to Will Gosling. He'll be the lordly man to tell you about that.' William Matthew Gosling is a second-generation Suffolk man who has lived in Burton all his life:

'Father was a Suffolk man. He lived at Belstead near Ipswich, though he was born at Creeting St Mary. At first he used to come up every winter to malt; and then he'd go back again in the summer months when the Burton men used to clean the maltings down. My father when he settled up here had only sixteen shillings a week. He was a wagoner for Bass's. He was single and got only sixteen shillings: the married men got eighteen. He got married up here and settled down. But

LEATHER MACHINISTS, WALSALL

he never lost his accent. I can remember to this day when I took my father's dinner to the malthouse: as soon as I pushed the door open the first words I heard was: "Blast, bor, your nearly pulled thet door off!"

'But it was hard work. By gosh, it was hard work, needing good strong healthy men. I found that out myself. I mean there's chaps like myself – about twelve stone ten pounds – you were expected to carry bags of barley at sixteen stone four; and sometimes there wasn't a job for you in the hard days when there was a lot of men out of work. And there was one boss – well, if he couldn't spell your name you'd had it. You'd got to go! I remember one man called Paternoster: that's a good old Suffolk name. Yes, there wasn't a job for you if you couldn't carry the barley. It was all manhandled in those days. About eight men and a foreman had to get 300 quarters of barley off the wagons for a day's work. You had to do, that's your day's money. And the biggest – the biggest godsend that ever came to Bass's in the maltings was the endless belt. It used to carry the barley to where you wanted it instead of you having to carry it on your shoulders. I've come home once or twice with blood coming from my back-collar stud-band and my shoulder bones. You know, the skin rubbed off with carrying the barley. It was awful! I reckon it was the hardest job next to coal-mining. And coal-mining was only worse

through the danger of it being underground. I've gone home at nights with clothes drenched with sweat from head to foot and the wife has had to pull my socks off, they've been that wet inside my boots. That was the heat of the kilns.

'When I was at Bass's they used to soak the barley for three days, and then it was turned on to the floors. It was divided between three floors. Then it was spread out on the floors to grow. Bass's method was to try and get as much root out of the corn before the stalk came out at the other end of the grain. Of course it wasn't always possible, but Bass had a method of doing it for which they got a very well-known name for making malt. And they relied on all these old Suffolk chaps that came up to do the work. Then when the barley was put on the kiln it stopped on the kiln for four days, starting from about 130 degrees Fahrenheit the first day, 140–50 the second day, 160–70 the third, and up to the required heat for the fourth day. With the strong ale beer, the very dark, it used to run to 215–18 degrees.'

James Knights of Suffolk described what happened to the malt afterwards. This was at an earlier period when methods were primitive even by the standards of a decade later:

'The malt came off the floor and it would go into a garner, and then it all had to be screened. They did this on the screens they called *Joe and Charlie* – two big screens. You'd get your

REBUILDING THE MALTINGS AFTER A FIRE, WOOD STREET, BURTON ON TRENT

BURTON MALTSTERS

good barley and the muck would go behind the screens. You had to throw the malted barley up against the screen. It was done by a fan as well. It was hot: it would nearly kill you. We had to have masks for this. When it had been screened you'd got to be in there and the malted barley would come out of a big hole just big enough to get a comb-sack through; and it used to run into a big heap; and you'd got to be inside there a-throwing on it back so it didn't bung up the hole. When you come out of there you was drunk from the dust of the malt – without having nawthen to drink! No, you didn't want anything to drink. You was drunk. When you come out of this you was absolutely drunk! Then if you'd lie down for a few minutes, have a few minutes' sleep, you were right again.

'For the work we used to do up there we used to have all the beer we could drink. There used to be a chap told off every day to fetch us beer in two nine-quart cans. I often had eight or nine pints before breakfast; and breakfast was at eight o'clock, when we used to get to work at two o'clock in the morning. You never got drunk from that: you were used to it and you always had it. Sweated it out turning the barley and turning the malt. But it was all rush and go: one to beat the other. Of course that was three storey high: a floor here, then the next floor, then the top floor. Three floors in a malt-house. One floor would be up against another.'

This competition between the men working on different

floors was confirmed by many of the maltsters. The men on one floor would complain, for instance, that they had a thicker *piece* of barley to turn than the men on the floor above them: 'The top floor is not spread as thick as this 'un', and so on. It was harder, therefore, to turn, and since they were on piece-work they were afraid it would affect their wage.

*George Ewart Evans*

using a bodkin to clear the holes. We used to work down a row of bricks or tiles. We got a penny for each brick, and it was a wonderful thing for us to earn some money during the school holidays. We also used to catch greenfinches that came on to the barley. We caught them with a net and we used to sell them as cage-birds.'

*George Ewart Evans*

## GWENDOLINE'S KNITTING NEEDLE

In the close season after the malting finished, the buildings were cleaned down thoroughly. One of the essential jobs was to clean the perforated kiln-bricks or tiles. I first head about this job from Mrs Gwendoline Hancock of Ipswich. For this she used a bent knitting needle with a cork to protect her hand. Tom Wood of Burton described the process: 'During the school holidays we used to go *kill-pricking*. We used to prick out the holes in the malting tiles. They'd get fouled up with barley and dust during the malting season. Through these holes the hot air rose from the *kill* underneath and roasted the barley, so they had to be clear. When we were kill-pricking we used to put a sack down on the floor and lie on our bellies

## WILLIAM DENNY – MALTSTER

'I first went to Burton when I was nineteen. I worked on the farm before I went up there. I was fit and strong and I wouldn't be messed about by anyone. The hours on the farm were six-thirty to five-thirty in the summer; seven o'clock till five o'clock in the winter. But you'd do a haysel and a harvest and perhaps they didn't want you after that. So I signed on for Burton at the Ipswich *Railway Hotel*. I signed on a Thursday and my ticket was waiting for me at Ipswich Station ready to go up on the Monday. My first job was in the store, a-bushelling barley, putting the barley into sacks, doing the carrying jobs and so on. Store-room work they called it. They paid you twenty-one shillings a week for a six-day week. The

QUEEN STREET, WOLVERHAMPTON

store chaps didn't work on Sundays but they stood by in case one of the regular maltsters was away from work. Then I went into the maltings. For this I got four shillings a day, five for Sunday. If you came any morning an hour or so early – you had to do sometimes – you got a shilling extra. If you got through your malting season you got fourpence a day as well as your wage. Some called it holiday money. This was added to your last pay before you came home. I recollect in my first year I got £2 4s 2d: the extra tuppence was for a half-day I stood in for a mate of mine.

'In the maltings the grain was taken up from the bottom floor by the scuttles – through the loading holes. I recollect that thirty years after I left Burton I went back on a visit with my son – we were returning from North Wales – and we saw a foreman called Smith who was there in my time. This man told my son: "No one could handle the scuttles better than your father." I aren't a boasting man but it was the truth, and it was good to hear it.

'After coming home from work and having some tea we'd go round the town, having a pint at one pub and then at another. There was the *Wheatsheaf, Punch Bowl, Golden Ball* and many more. We were a crowd together and we used to enjoy ourselves. We used to sing, and one thing we used to do up there was to step-dance on top of a barrel. In all the pubs

up there you could get a free clay-pipe at that time – with the pub's name on it. After my first season in Burton I recollect I brought ninety clay-pipes home with me. We were in lodgings, most of us, paying twelve shillings a week. Some got on well, but we didn't. I once lodged in Canal Street, and a sixteen-year-old girl looked after the meals for me and another chap named Stover. I had a fancy for something tasty, and one night I gave her a pig's fry and asked her to cook it for us the next day. When we came home it was hardly warmed let alone cooked. The girl wasn't there when we ate it, and didn't we swear! I was courting one of the Burton girls. Her named was Good or Wood – I forget now. She was a nice girl and I bought her a pair of shoes. But her mother noticed her new shoes and asked her where they come from; and when the girl couldn't give a good account of the shoes her mother chopped the heels off! Talking about girls, there was a man up there in the maltings, a piece-worker called Runnacles. This one was strict and made us work. But one day he say to me he knew Ashbocking where I come from. He was a-courting a girl there. But I was right surprised when he told me the name o' the girl because I knew her; she had a face like a bullace pudding gone wrong!

'Bass used to give us a piece of beef at Christmas at that time – 1901 it was when I first went up. They used to give six

GREENGATE STREET, STAFFORD

pounds for the single chaps and ten pounds for the married ones. It was good beef, too. Some of the chaps used to sell it; some of 'em used to send it home to Suffolk. I gave a bit of it to my Burton landlady. But you needed suthen like beef. You didn't go up to Burton for a holiday!

'The job was slavery. One year I remember I was taken bad, and I couldn't go on and I went to see the doctor. He was an Irishman, and as soon as I went into his sargery he say to me: "You don't want to tell me what's the matter with you. Bass's pick up the young chaps and bring you up here from the country and they work you to *dead*!"

'We used to finish at the maltings towards the end of May. But before you went home you had to have a new suit. You dussn't come home from Burton wearing the suit you went up in. I used to buy my suit at a Burton shop called Tarver's. I believe it's still in the town. The suit had what we used to call a *donkey-dealer's* jacket. It was cut long, half-way down your thigh, and it buttoned up tight almost up to your neck. It had a long centre-vent at the back and a shaped waist with a couple o' buttons. You could get a good suit with a good style of cloth for £2 10s. One regular thing, too, before you came back home was to buy a teapot. I recollect I bought one to take home to a family I was lodging with in Suffolk. My Burton landlady say to me: "Aren't you going to give me the

teapot?" but I told her I was a-taking it hoom to Suffolk. It was a rare teapot; it held about six pints and they made them at Woodville just outside Burton. When I got it hoom the old lady I was a-staying with was as pleased as a cat with nine cocks.

*George Ewart Evans*

## UTTOXETER

During the past twelve months a large amount of money has been raised in Uttoxeter, far beyond the usual appeals the public have been asked to contribute, towards the expenses of improving the whole of the schools in the town, in order to meet the requirements of the Education Department. A purse of 100 sovereigns was presented to the Vicar (the Revd H. Abud) on his return from the Hawaiian Islands, after an absence of twelve months. The scarcity of water in the town caused the Sanitary Authority to press forward a new water scheme. The Bramshall supply being found insufficient, the Somersal springs were tapped and a week or two ago the water was turned on for the town. The event was hailed with joy by all the inhabitants, who had suffered for a long time from a

CIRCUS PARADE, UTTOXETER

scarcity of water. Two serious fires broke out during the year, one at Denstone College and the other at Fole Mills, the latter being burnt to the ground. These two calamities led to the purchasing of a new steam fire-engine. An appeal was made by the Lighting and Watching Inspectors, and so generously was the scheme subscribed to that in a very short time £600 was collected towards this object. The inauguration and public dinner which followed proved quite a 'red-letter' day in local annals. The science classes held under the auspices of the County Council have been productive of much good. They have been well attended, and the students have been very successful in their examinations. Taken as a whole, the trade of the town may be considered good, the firm of Messrs Bamford and Sons being still well to the fore. The farmers of the district have been the worst sufferers, stock and farming produce of all kinds being exceedingly low in price.

*Stafford Advertiser, 'Events 1894'*

## WALKING HOME WITH SUNDAY

The canal, which ran north and south, reflected a blue and white sky. Towards the bridge, from the north came a long narrow canal-boat roofed with tarpaulins; and towards the bridge, from the south came a similar craft, sluggishly creeping. The towing-path was a morass of sticky brown mud, for in the way of rain that year was breaking the records of a century and a half. Thirty yards in front of each boat an unhappy skeleton of a horse floundered its best in the quagmire. The honest endeavour of one of the animals received a frequent tonic from a bare-legged girl of seven who heartily curled a whip about its crooked large-jointed legs. The ragged and filthy child danced in the rich mud round the horse's flanks with the simple joy of one who had been rewarded for good behaviour by the unrestricted use of a whip for the first time.

Edwin, with his elbows on the stone parapet of the bridge, stared uninterested at the spectacle of the child, the whip, and the skeleton. He was not insensible to the piquancy of the pageant life, but his mind was preoccupied with grave and heavy matters. He had left school that day, and what his eyes

HORSE SALE, BALANCE STREET, UTTOXETER

GUILD STREET, BURTON ON TRENT

FORSBROOK

DIMMINGSDALE, NEAR CHEADLE

saw as he leaned on the bridge was not a willing beast and a gladdened infant, but the puzzling world and the advance guard of its problems bearing down on him. Slim, gawky, untidy, fair, with his worn black-braided clothes, and slung over his shoulders in a bursting satchel the last load of his schoolbooks, and on his bright, rough hair a shapeless cap whose lining protruded behind, he had the extraordinary wistful look of innocence and simplicity which marks most boys of sixteen. It seemed rather a shame, it seemed even tragic, that this naïve, simple creature, with his straightforward and friendly eyes so eager to believe appearance, this creature immaculate of worldly experience, must soon be transformed into a man, wary, incredulous, detracting. Older eyes might have wept at the simplicity of those eyes.

This picture of Edwin as a wistful innocent would have made Edwin laugh. He had been seven years at school, and considered himself a hardened sort of brute, free of illusions. And he sometimes thought that he could judge the world better than most neighbouring mortals.

'Hello! The Sunday!' he murmured, without turning his eyes.

Another boy, a little younger and shorter, and clothed in a superior untidiness, had somehow got on to the bridge, and

96

SNOW HILL, SHELTON

was leaning with his back against the parapet which supported Edwin's elbows. His eyes were franker and simpler even than the eyes of Edwin, and his lips seemed to be permanently parted in a good-humoured smile. His name was Charlie Orgreave, but at school he was invariably called 'the Sunday' – not 'Sunday,' but 'the Sunday' – and nobody could authoritatively explain how he had come by the nickname. Its origin was lost in the prehistoric ages of his childhood. He and Edwin had been chums for several years. They had not sworn fearful oaths of loyalty; they did not constitute a secret society; they had not even pricked forearms and written certain words in blood; for these rites are only performed at Harrow, and possibly at the Oldcastle High School, which imitates Harrow. Their fellowship meant chiefly that they spent a great deal of time together, instinctively and unconsciously enjoying each other's mere presence, and that in public arguments they always reinforced each other, whatever the degree of intellectual dishonesty thereby necessitated.

'I'll bet you mine gets to the bridge first,' said the Sunday. With an ingenious movement of the shoulders he arranged himself so that the parapet should bear the weight of his satchel.

Edwin Clayhanger slowly turned round, and perceived that the object which the Sunday had appropriated as 'his' was the other canal-boat, advancing from the south.

'Horse or boat?' asked Edwin.

'Boat's nose, of course,' said the Sunday.

'Well,' said Edwin, having surveyed the unconscious competitors, and counting on the aid of the whipping child. 'I don't mind laying you five.'

RUDYARD

CRATEMAKERS IN THE POTTERIES

BACK-TO-BACKS

'That be damned for a tale!' protested the Sunday. 'We said we'd never bet less than ten — you know that.'

'Yes, but —' Edwin hesitatingly drawled.

'But what?'

'All right. Ten,' Edwin agreed. 'But it's not fair. You've got a rare start on me.'

'Rats!' said the Sunday, with finality. In the pronunciation of this word the difference between his accent and Edwin's came out clear. The Sunday's accent was less local; there was a hint of a short 'e' sound in the 'a', and a briskness about the consonants, that Edwin could never have compassed. The Sunday's accent was as carelessly superior as his clothes. Evidently the Sunday had some one at home who had not learnt the art of speech in the Five Towns.

He began to outline a scheme, in which perpendicular expectoration figured, for accurately deciding the winner, and a complicated argument might have ensued about this, had it not soon become apparent that Edwin's boat was going to be handsomely beaten, despite the joyous efforts of the little child. The horse that would die but would not give up, was only saved from total subsidence at every step by his indomitable if aged spirit. Edwin handed over the ten marbles even before the other boat had arrived at the bridge.

'Here,' he said. 'And you may as well have these, too,' adding five more to the ten, all he possessed. They were not

THE CLARION CLUB, HANLEY

the paltry marble of to-day, plaything of infants, but the majestic 'rinker', black with white spots, the king of marbles in an era when whole populations practised the game. Edwin looked at them half regretfully as they lay in the Sunday's hands. They seemed prodigious wealth in those hands, and he felt somewhat as a condemned man might feel who bequeaths his jewels on the scaffold. Then there was a rattle, and a tumour grew out larger on the Sunday's thigh.

The winning boat, long preceded by its horse, crawled under the bridge and passed northwards to the sea, laden with crates of earthenware. And then the loser, with the little girl's father and mother and her brothers and sisters, and her kitchen, drawing-room, and bedroom, and her smoking chimney and her memories and all that was hers, in the stern of it, slid beneath the boys' downturned faces while the whip cracked away beyond the bridge. They could see, between the whitened tarpaulins, that the deep belly of the craft was filled with clay.

'Where does that there clay come from?' asked Edwin. For not merely was he honestly struck by a sudden new curiosity, but it was meet for him to behave like a man now, and to ask manly questions.

'Runcorn,' said the Sunday scornfully. 'Can't you see it painted all over the boat?'

'Why do they bring clay all the way from Runcorn?'

'They don't bring it from Runcorn. They bring it from

Cornwall. It comes round by sea – see?' He laughed.

'Who told you?' Edwin roughly demanded.

'Anybody knows that!' said the Sunday grandly, but always maintaining his gay smile.

'Seems devilish funny to me,' Edwin murmured, after reflection, 'that they should bring clay all that roundabout way just to make crocks of it here. Why should they choose just *this* place to make crocks in? I always understood —'

'Oh! Come *on*!' the Sunday cut him short. 'It's blessed well one o'clock and after!'

They climbed the long bank from the canal up to the Manor Farm, at which high point their roads diverged, one path leading direct to Bleakridge where Orgreave lived, and the other zig-zagging down through neglected pasturage into Bursley proper. Usually they parted here without a word, taking pride in such Spartan taciturnity, and they would doubtless have done the same this morning also, though it were fiftyfold their last walk together as two schoolboys. But an incident intervened.

'Hold on!' cried the Sunday.

To the south of them, a mile and a half off, in the wreathing mist of the Cauldon Bar Ironworks, there was a yellow gleam that even the capricious sunlight could not kill, and then two rivers of fire sprang from the gleam and ran in a thousand delicate and lovely hues down the side of a mountain of refuse. They were emptying a few tons of molten slag at the Cauldon

ARNOLD BENNETT AND FAMILY, COBRIDGE

Bar Ironworks. The two rivers hung slowly dying in the mists of smoke. They reddened and faded, and you thought they had vanished, and you could see them yet, and then they escaped the baffled eye, unless a cloud aided them for a moment against the sun; and their ephemeral but enchanting beauty had expired for ever.

'Now!' said Edwin sharply.

'One minute ten seconds,' said the Sunday, who had snatched out his watch, an inestimable contrivance with a centre-seconds hand. 'By Jove! That was a good 'un.'

A moment later two smaller boys, both laden with satchels, appeared over the brow from the canal.

'Let's wait a jiff,' said the Sunday to Edwin, and as the smaller boys showed no hurry he bawled out to them across the intervening cinder-waste: 'Run!' They ran. They were his younger brothers, Johnnie and Jimmie. 'Take this and hook it!' he commanded, passing the strap of his satchel over his head as they came up. In fatalistic silence they obeyed the smiling tyrant.

'What are you going to do?' Edwin asked.

'I'm coming down your way a bit.'

'But I thought you said you were peckish.'

'I shall eat three slices of beef instead of my usual brace,' said

the Sunday carelessly.

Edwin was touched. And the Sunday was touched, because he knew he had touched Edwin. After all, this was a solemn occasion. But neither would overtly admit that its solemnity had affected him. Hence, first one and then the other began to skim stones with vicious force over the surface of the largest of the three ponds that gave interest to the Manor Farm. When they had thus proved to themselves that the day differed in no manner from any other breaking-up day, they went forward.

On their left were two pitheads whose double wheels revolved rapidly in smooth silence, and the puffing engine-house and all the trucks and gear of a large ironstone mine. On their right was the astonishing farm, with barns and ricks and cornfields complete, seemingly quite unaware of its forlorn oddness in that foul arena of manufacture. In front, on a little hill in the vast valley, was spread out the Indian-red architecture of Bursley – tall chimneys and rounded ovens, schools, the new scarlet market, the grey tower of the old church, the high spire of the evangelical church, the low spire of the church of genuflexions, and the crimson chapels, and rows of little red houses with amber chimney-pots, and the gold angel of the blackened Town Hall topping the whole. The sedate reddish browns and reds of the compositions, all

FACTORY GIRLS

netted in flowing scarves of smoke, harmonized exquisitely with the chill blues of the chequered sky. Beauty was achieved, and none saw it.

The boys descended without a word through the brick-strewn pastures, where a horse or two cropped the short grass. At the railway bridge, which carried a branch mineral line over the path, they exchanged a brief volley of words with the working-lads who always played pitch-and-toss there in the dinner-hour; and the Sunday added to the collection of shawds and stones lodged on the under ledges of the low iron girders. A strange boy, he had sworn to put ten thousand stones on those ledges before he died, or perish in the attempt. Hence Edwin sometimes called him 'Old Perish-in-the-attempt'. A little farther on the open gates of a manufactory disclosed six men playing the noble game of rinkers on a smooth patch of ground near the weighing machine. These six men were Messieurs Ford, Carter, and Udall, the three partners owning the works, and three of their employees. They were celebrated marble-players, and the boys stayed to watch them as, bending with one knee almost touching the earth, they shot the rinkers from their stubby thumbs with a canon-like force and precision that no boy could ever hope to equal. 'By gum!' mumbled Edwin involuntarily, when an

HANLEY PARK

DECORATING CHINA

impossible shot was accomplished; and the bearded shooter, pleased by this tribute from youth, twisted his white apron into a still narrower ring round his waist. Yet Edwin was not thinking about the game. He was thinking about a battle that lay before him, and how he would be weakened in the fight by the fact that in the last school examination, Charlie Orgreave, younger than himself by a year, had ousted him from the second place in the school. The report in his pocket said: 'Position in class next term: third'; whereas he had been second since the beginning of the year. There would of course be no 'next term' for him, but the report remained. A youth who has come to grips with that powerful enemy, his father, cannot afford to be handicapped by even such a trifle as a report entirely irrelevant to the struggle.

Suddenly Charlie Orgreave gave a curt nod, and departed, in nonchalant good-humour, doubtless considering that to accompany his chum any farther would be to be guilty of girlish sentimentality. And Edwin nodded with equal curtness and made off slowly into the maze of Bursley. The thought in his heart was: 'I'm on my own, now. I've got to face it now, by myself.' And he felt that not merely his father, but the leagued universe, was against him.

*Arnold Bennett*

## HIGHLANDS AND HIGH SCHOOLS

Our horses found the steep hillside – bank is the local idiom – laborious; and, when they had pulled us to what we thought the top, they turned to a second portion as steep as the first. Indeed the road, to beyond Middle Hills, is almost continually up. My companion described the Churnet Valley on our right, and we observed moorland farmsteads set amid clumps of trees on the bleak hill sides. Presently we found ourselves immediately beneath, and then running along side, the Ramshaw Rocks, with a view on our left across the top of the Roches, and a panorama of Leek in the distance behind. We noticed all manner of weird and fantastic shapes along the skyline of the Rocks, and readily realised we were in the Highlands of North Stafford.

The Staffordshire Highlands, a vast expanse of grouse moor and stock-raising grass-land, are really the Southern Highlands of the Peak. They are intersected everywhere by hill and dale, and ever and anon adorned with massive rocks. The difference 'twixt the Northern hills and Southern heights of Peakland is apparent in the cliffs and fences, in the limestone of what he calls the Derby country, north and east of the Manifold, and the grit-stone across the Stafford and Cheshire borders; and in

BOARD SCHOOL COOKERY CLASS, LONGTON

this difference between lime and grit lies the secret of the rugged grandeur of North Stafford.

Ramshaw School, a bleak, plain-looking building on our left, just above the termination of the Rocks, considered as an educational establishment in this wild region, is worthy a passing glance. My companion has a winter picture from here, 'Playtime'.

Ah, Playtime! I trow we all remember playtime. Those few moments of sweetness sandwiched between hours of all manner of elementary monotony, from multiplication to the intricacies and irregularities of the verb 'to be'. The playtime which was denied us at the approach of examinations, or when the teacher, in his supreme autocracy, had arisen from the wrong side of his bed. Life then was not all one grand sweet song; but what would we not give for one short old-time playtime of innocent amusement and reckless abandonment, even if it should end in a swollen eye and an interview with the master. These sliding wenches make me morose. Poor little hussies; ye know not what woe the world is hoarding for ye!

*W.H. Nithsdale*

## SPINNING AND WEAVING AT LEEK

We saw boxes containing sewing silks of every conceivable colour, machine twists, embroidery silks, ties, trimmings, braids, bindings, beltings, buttons, laces, and even small initial letters for handkerchiefs – a truly wonderful assortment of Leek manufactures.

Through various departments and the large counting-house we passed into the mills and saw the first stages in the production of the spun and twist silks which are Leek's staple industries; work, by-the-way, a few years ago executed in the garrets of private houses.

The silk is imported in bales, and, after picking, the delicate threads are wound together from the banks stretched upon very light skeleton frames, 'swifts' they are called, to giant wooden bobbins, in a large airy mill containing many horizontal rows of frames and bobbins; some winding white silks from China and Japan; some very light fawn silks from Canton, and some bright yellow silks from Bengal.

A second room was devoted to silk doubling, multiplying the fine threads of silk by re-winding them into whatever number of threads may be required for producing the various sizes of silk, and giving a rough sort of twist over a circular

103

LEEK

drum running from one mammoth bobbin to another. Here, as in the mill devoted to winding, were rows of spinning drums and bobbins.

The twisting, on bobbins like nothing so much as the small boy's spinning top, but making full sixteen hundred revolutions per minute, was even more fascinating than the winding and doubling. This process was formerly carried out in long low 'shades', where the chief features in place of the tiers of spinning bobbins and one man tending hundreds, were a large spinning wheel worked by a male twister, and a small barefooted boy whose business it was to run the length of the 'shade' and back again drawing the wound threads of silk around pegs as he ran.

The twisted silks are now despatched to the dyers.

Proceeding to the weaving sheds, we found the dyed silks being woven on gigantic Jacquard looms into named ribbons, costume bands, coat hangers, boot webs and skirt labels in innumerable quantities. A Salvation Army ribbon, in regulation crimson silk with gold lettering, being particularly interesting. Numerous fine threads of crimson and gold were being drawn from separate spools by the clumsy looking weaving contrivance, through a cardboard pattern away up at the top, and all along the front of the long looms came the finished ribbons in the well known colours of 'Blood and Fire'.

Through a subway and the joiners' yard, we passed into another warehouse and saw girls deftly labelling and packing

reels of sewing silks. Through another subway – the firms mills are all connected by subways and we never got a spot of rain in all our rambling – we came to the braid sheds of the Fountain Street Mills. Here at small Jacquard looms, some worked by treadles and using hand shuttles, girls were weaving braid trimmings and silk ties in fantastic colours and pretty designs; and at one small machine a girl was rapidly converting yard after yard of plain ribbon into fancy bands for millinery trimmings.

Hence, we looked into the printing and lithographic department, where Messrs Brough print their own labels, pattern cards and such like articles; and then by another subway were conducted to the spooling room. Here girls sat before small machines at steel tables, tared the reels on small brass scales, fixed the reels in the machines and rapidly spooled the running thread backwards and forwards until the reels were filled to the requisite weights.

In the next department velvet skirt trimmings and bindings, collars and embroideries were being made. Items here were sewing machines by the dozen with skilful girls working with bewildering rapidity, while younger lasses were engaged making fasteners for ladies' dress pockets.

Another room was set apart for the making of immense quantities of cardboard boxes. The principal features being cardboard, guillotines and paste; and wonderful glueing machines, where paper travelled over rollers to be cut and dabbed on all sides of the boxes with marvellous skill and

MANIFOLD VALLEY RAILWAY

dexterity. Some small girls armed with enormous brushes amused us considerably.

*W.H. Nithsdale*

## BURTON BEER

Burton beer makes me blythe, French wines make me sick,
I'm devoted to ale, and to ale I will stick.
Henceforth let the grape to the barleycorn bow,
Here's success to the farmer, and speed to the plough.

*Anon.*

## LEEK POST OFFICE

Deliveries begin at 7 a.m., 11.30, and 4 p.m. Letters are also received from London at 9 a.m., and a bag containing correspondence, from all parts is received from Stoke at 9.15 a.m., and 6.20 p.m., delivery of which is limited to callers. Sundays at 7 a.m. only. For despatches the Letter Box closes at 8.30 for the Potteries and the North; 9.35 for Manchester, Lancashire and Yorkshire; 11.10 for London and the South; 12.50 for Manchester and the North; 3.30 for Crewe and Stoke; and 7.45 for all parts; on Sunday 7.30 p.m., only.

Letters posted up to 8.30 are delivered in London after 4 p.m., and up to 11.10 are delivered in the London District after 6 p.m.

Letters posted up to 7.45 p.m., are delivered in Manchester at 7 a.m.; up to 9.35 a.m., are delivered in Manchester at 12.15 p.m., and up to 12.50 p.m., are delivered in Manchester at 3.30 p.m.

Letters for the Potteries posted up to 3.30 p.m. are delivered the same day.

Letters for Macclesfield up to 12.50 p.m. are delivered at 4.30 p.m.

Registered Letters must be presented not later than 30 minutes before the Letter Box closes.

Letters posted with an additional stamp up to 7.55 p.m. (Sundays excepted) will be sent by the departing mail.

On Bank Holidays, Christmas Day, and Good Friday, there is only one delivery, and only one night despatch.

Rural Postmen are despatched at 6 a.m. to Cheddleton, Butterton, Horton, Onecote-over-Bradnop, Meerbrook, Rudyard, Grindon, Winkhill and Waterfall. Letters for Longsdon, Endon and Wetley Rocks are delivered from Stoke-on-Trent.

Money Orders, Postal Orders and Savings Bank, business is transacted at the Head Offices 7 a.m. to 8 p.m. on week days. Town Sub-Offices 8 a.m. to 8 p.m.

Telegraph Office open daily from 8 a.m. to 8 p.m., except on Sundays, when it is open from 8 a.m. to 10 p.m. only.

Town Sub-Offices are now open at West Street (Money Orders and Savings Bank), Ball Haye Green, Mill Street, Portland Street and Broad Street.

Pillar Boxes are in the Cattle Market, Abbotts Lane, Compton, Ball Haye Green, Ball Haye Street, Mill Street,

RUDYARD LAKE, LEEK

Railway Station, St Edward Street and Stockwell Street.

Inland Parcels Post – Parcels are forwarded to all places in the British Isles at rates as follows: – First pound 3d., every additional pound up to 10lbs., 1d. a pound. Dimensions not to exceed 3ft. 6in. in length, length and girth combined not to exceed 6ft. Dangerous articles are not carried. Parcels must not be posted as letters, but handed in. Parcels so posted will be treated as letters. To insure compensation for loss or damage to a parcel, a certificate of posting should be obtained when handed in.

*The Leek Annual, 1898*

## THE MISSED BUTT

*There is a superstition current in North Staffordshire (if elsewhere, I am unacquainted with the fact) which holds – or did hold a generation back – that if a farmer, in sowing his yearly breadth, accidentally misses or overlooks one of the 'butts', a circumstance which occasionally happens, and does not perceive the omission till the absence of the green blade discovers the fact, it is a sure sign of a death in his household.*

*The 'butts', in the North Staffordshire vernacular, are the long narrow ridges, or beds, thrown together by the plough, with separating furrows for the drainage on which the seed is sown.*

I was Teamsman for that year
Tho' but slim and over-grown:
Father did the sowing then.
All the yearly breadth was sown,

Save an angle of a field,
Lately broken up from lea –
That where stood the old sheepcote
By the lightning-splintered tree.

Night was down upon us; yet
Father coughed and firked his beard;
'Twas not much – the mould was dry –
Seed was down – the team was geared.

Then he skyward looked, where winds,
Clouds, and rain were gathering might –
'Up, my lads!' he said; 'we'll do't
Ere we stable for the night:

''Tis o'er late a week or more
Now – and every sign of rain;
We may wish it done i'th' morn,'
So we slapped to work again.

106

COMPTON FARM

Flew the harrows o'er the loam;
Flew the seed from flying fist.
But when springing blades showed green
Then 'twas found a butt was missed!

'I have farmed for forty year,
Sown my seed myself a score,'
Said my father; 'but I never,
Never played this game afore.'

Then up spake a wrinkled crone,
''Tis a deadly certain sign;
There will be a death i'th' house
Ere the Christmas berries shine.'

Then the household laughed aloud,
Lightly chode the dame, and said
''Twas a weak old woman's tale:'
But the woman shook her head.

All the family after that
Scanned the butt with dubious eye,
Felt a sinking at their hearts,
Probing not for reason why.

Came disease when fields had flowers,
Breathed upon a lassie fair,
Stole her music, laid her dead –
Dead among her glory hair!

Bare and barren stretched the butt
Just as if the need were less;
Dead and still our darling lay
With no want we might redress.

Dropped the silence on the earth,
Came the ripeness to the corn;
And the reapers went about,
And the crowded fields were shorn.

Sadly eyed we all the butt,
Hinting never aught; and yet
Through the years that barren butt
No one of us may e'er forget.

*George Heath*

ROYAL SCHOOL ORPHANAGE, WOLVERHAMPTON

## WOLVERHAMPTON ORPHANAGE

On our arrival at the Orphanage yesterday, we were received by Mr Hamblett, and directly introduced to Miss Amsden, the kind and obliging lady superintendent, who takes just pride in showing visitors over the institution, in which daily life proceeds with the regularity of clockwork, and where everything is kept in apple pie order. All through the motto seems to be, 'A place for everything, and everything in its place'. This applies throughout – school-rooms, dining-halls, and dormitories, right down to the scullery and to the rooms in which the children keep their slippers and black their boots. With the two officials named we commenced our lengthy tour of inspection. It should be mentioned that there are at present in the Orphan Asylum 150 boys and 100 girls. There is no mixing of the sexes – there are separate schoolrooms, play-rooms, play grounds, dining halls, and boys and girls never see each other except on special occasions, and when they journey together to St Paul's Church on the Sabbath. We first made the acquaintance of the girls in their schoolroom, and had the pleasure of seeing them go through a wonderful exercise in calisthenics, or chest expanding, muscle extending, musical drill. Miss Hitchings, one of the assistant governesses, an accomplished pianist, seated herself at the instrument and played the strains to which the girls who formed up on the floor of the schoolroom, and taking the lead from one of the

governesses, extended their arms and hands in graceful movement. It was the very poetry of motion; no regiment of the line ever flashed their sabres with more perfect precision. Then the girlish forms, in sober coloured frocks and spotless white pinafores, closed up, and still obeying the martial music, marched and counter-marched, moved in and out in intricate maze-like movements with faultless steadiness, closed up again, advanced like a solid wall of happy contented faces, and then filed off in twos to resume their scholastic studies. These physical exercises form one of the features of the institution, and conduce in no small measure to the healthiness of both boys and girls. Indeed at the moment there is not a single patient in the infirmary with its 25 beds, which says much for the observance of the laws of health and sanitation at the institution. By and bye we were privileged to hear a number of the younger girls – bright smiling little dots – sing a couple of action songs to pianoforte accompaniment. He must indeed be a soulless being who could listen unmoved to those little fatherless ones, lisping their lullabies. While Miss Hitchings played, they sang about 'Invalid dolly', folding their pinafores into make-believe dolls, rocking them whilst they sang sweet and low, then in the same soothing air crooning over them with a gentle hum as musicals the sound of bees amid summer flowers.

Outside their studies there is ample evidence that the girls are

MUSIC LESSONS, ROYAL SCHOOL ORPHANAGE, WOLVERHAMPTON

well trained in domestic work. They are gradually given a sure foundation in cookery, needlework, laundry work, and other household duties, and in every direction in which it can reasonably be done their services are utilised. It was pleasant as passing along to see a number of girls busily plying their needles in the mending room, under the care of a teacher, while in another room several were busily engaged in more responsible sewing duties. Elsewhere we came upon several girls engaged at pianos, taking their music lessons. To prevent misapprehension, it should be explained that when the friends or relatives of any of the inmates wish them to learn music, the cost of the instruction comes out of their own pockets, and not out of the ordinary funds. In the Cambridge Local Examinations last year, one Orphanage girl was distinguished for music, and three were highly commended. In this connection, it should be mentioned that two girls were also distinguished in Scripture. Before saying farewell to the girls we ought to mention that Miss Amsden in her duties is ably assisted by Miss Stuart, who is also sewing mistress, while the head assistant governess is Miss Pearce, her assistants being Miss Davies, Miss Hitchings, Miss R. Walton, and Miss G. Sargent. Some of these ladies have themselves grown up within the walls of the institution, and have rewarded Miss Amsden for her fostering care by showing their capability to undertake the responsible duties which have been entrusted to them. Their

attachment to the 'home', as the Orphanage is called, is as sacred as the tie that binds the most fortunate of sons and daughters to the paternal roof.

A word or two about the boys. They are a bonny, bright, intelligent set of little fellows, all looking the picture of good health, and with happiness and contentment written on every countenance. They are a credit to the institution, and to the painstaking and scholarly head master, Mr A.T. Hawes, and his assistants, Mr L.F. Stiles, Mr J. Robinson, and Mr W.H. Crump. As we enter the school-room, which, like all the other apartments of the institution, is spacious, with plenty of elbow room and good ventilation, we are struck by the excellent training and discipline of the lads. Mr Hamblett has been singing their praises as we move along and telling of their scholastic successes, and now we find them, large and small boys, engaged in a drawing lesson. Drawing is a great feature of the curriculum. A general idea of the educational work of the institution is furnished in the last annual report of the Board of Managers. It states that the work done during the year on 'broad and practical lines had been very satisfactory',and adds: 'The boys were examined in May last by the Science and Art Department in mathematics, geology, physiography, and practical plain and solid geometry. Two obtained honours and were classed seventh and tenth, and for

LONGNOR

age first and second in the kingdom. Thirteen gained first and 78 second-class certificates, and one boy obtained a certificate for thorough knowledge and efficiency in shorthand, a subject which is now included in the education of the boys, with most gratifying results. Drawing is again classed as excellent.' It is worthy of record, too, that one boy, aged 14, was in the above examination bracketed seventh with a schoolmaster of the mature age of 38 years. Shorthand has been introduced by Mr Hamblett, who is himself a skilful stenographer. The results of the examinations reflect credit on Mr Hawes, and the fact that the schools are carried on entirely without corporal punishment is a feather in his cap as a disciplinarian. But about the drawing lesson. About 40 little boys were, with pencils and scale rules, engaged upon the construction of triangles, rhomboids, parallelograms, &c., and all appeared to be taking delight in bringing the geometrical outlines as near to a state of perfection as possible. Another class were engaged in memory drawing, others were deep in model and freehand drawing, and so on until we reached the most advanced boys, who presented some excellent specimens for our inspection. Directly the hour for dismissal arrived, and the boys trooped off in the merriest possible mood to get ready for tea. There are, by the way, spacious play rooms indoors for both boys and girls, with plenty of means for dumb-bell and other gymnastic exercises. Outside there is a fine large open playground, a

tennis ground recently extended for the girls, and within sight of the boys' dormitories is the six-acre cricket and football field. The Orphanage possesses a large and excellently appointed swimming bath, laid with enamelled bricks, and both boys and girls are taught swimming.

The exigencies of space forbid us entering into details as we should like as to the admirable method which characterises all the arrangements of the Charity. In the lavatories each child has a separate wash-basin, brush and comb, and towel, numbered with the child's own particular number; their lockers, slippers, boots, clothing, &c, are all identified in the same manner, and in the airy and scrupulously clean and lofty dormitories each little bedstead with its cosy, warm-looking coverlet, is numbered. Side by side they run in serried rows the full length of the dormitories, and at the end are the sleeping apartments of the officials who keep their charges company in their sleeping as well as in their waking hours. Daily life at the Orphanage is an unceasing round of activity. In summer the children rise at six, and in winter at 6.30, and they are always tucked safely in their little beds at 8 p.m. There are, of course, morning and evening prayers, then follow private studies, breakfast, school, and so on, the daily round of duty being run with unfailing regularity. The food placed before the children is of the best quality, and the larger,

PAWNBROKER, BURSLEM

cooking kitchens, and laundry are all worthy of inspection. Idleness is banished, the children having to black their own boots, make their own beds, and busy themselves usefully in spare moments. Wastefulness is not tolerated, and the spare crumbs and crusts of to-day become the bread and butter puddings of to-morrow.

Now let us dispel an illusion. It is a mistake to suppose that the Orphanage is too rich and prosperous. The balance-sheet for 1892 shows that the expenditure exceeds the present permanent income and annual subscriptions combined by £600 a year. There is plenty of room for more children if the funds would warrant their admission, and although the Orphanage has many generous friends, there is a pressing need for additional support, either by donations or annual subscriptions, in order that the usefulness of a splendid and economically managed institution may be extended. The highest of Christian work is ever being carried on within its walls, and what sweeter reward could benevolent men and women wish for than the consciousness of having assisted hapless orphans to fight the battle of life, and of having earned for themselves the Divine encomium associated with the text over the Orphanage portals – 'Inasmuch as ye did it unto one of these . . . ye did it unto me.'

*Midland Evening News, December 8, 1893*

UTTOXETER MARKET

WOLVERHAMPTON UNION WORKHOUSE

## TREAT FOR THE WOLVERHAMPTON WORKHOUSE CHILDREN

Those poor children who suffer the unhappy lot destined for the third and fourth generation of misguided parents, who, though born in adversity, are brought up in moral and Christian understandings at the Wolverhampton Workhouse, are not altogether forsaken by the outside world. There are those in the town who have for them no mere lip sympathy, but have sympathy of heart, which finds issue in practical deeds of kindliness, and which are never forgotten by the recipients, and never regretted by the doer of good works. Amongst them are several Guardians of the Poor, who take what might be called more than 'visiting' interest in the children committed to their care. Chief amongst them must be mentioned Mr Jacob J. Tate, through whose instrumentality the little ones were last summer treated to a glorious outing in the beautiful grounds adjoining his residence near Dunstall Park. This, the first holiday of the kind, was so thoroughly successful, that it was determined to make it an annual event. Thursday was the day fixed for the second treat, and at two o'clock the youngsters started from their big home in Bilston Road in brakes. They were driven direct to Mr Tate's grounds, the drum and fife band playing lively tunes *en route*. In the green fields they romped about with the freedom and rapture of birds released from long imprisonment in the cage – not that they never go outside the house, but so delightful was the change that they forgot 'the daily round, the common task', and the dull walls of their parish

home, and lost themselves completely in the pleasures of the moment. Not only did Mr and Mrs Tate subscribe to their happiness, but others helped in various ways to make the day a memorable one, amongst them being the Revd S. Cordon, Mr and Mrs J.F. Jones, Mr T.D. Greensill (chairman of the Board of Guardians), Mr and Mrs Cousins, Mr and Mrs Shepherd, Mr and Mrs L. Johnson, Mr and Mrs Plant, Mr J. Griffith, Mr and Mrs S. Craddock, together with Mr Mead (head master), the schoolmasters and mistresses from the house, and other officials. The family, which numbered close upon 200, were overwhelmed with kind words and deeds. Football was a favourite game with the boys and several gentlemen joined either side to their intense amusement. They engaged in their races, in fact, in all their games, making the little ones feel that they were not alone, but that there were some good people outside who loved them and were not too great to talk to them and play with them. It was really a right merry time that they had. Numerous prizes, contributed by the company, were competed for, and those whose physical infirmities prevented them engaging in the sports were not overlooked by the considerate eye of the judge. A sumptuous tea was provided, and towards eight o'clock the children gave three hearty cheers for Mr and Mrs Tate for their unbounded hospitality, and returned to their home the better and the brighter for their invigorating holiday. Mr and Mrs Tate also entertained a large party at their residence, including those above mentioned.

*Express and Star July 25, 1890*

DRYING YARD, STAFFORD LAUNDRY

## FAIR PLAY FOR THE HUNT

*Swynnerton Park, Stone, January 13th, 1886*

Dear Sir,

By desire of the Marquis of Stafford and the Committee of the North Stafford Hunt, I have to beg your kind attention to the dangerous and increasing practice of laying strands of wire along quick fences, and in other situations where their presence cannot be readily detected by a horseman. Numerous accidents, some of them fatal, have already occurred from this cause in various parts of the country. I feel sure, therefore, that you will pardon my expressing the earnest hope of the Hunt, that you will do all in your power to prevent the use of wire in the above-named way, and to have it removed in places where it already exists and where it is especially dangerous.

The Hunt would also feel much indebted to you if you would discourage the use of *barbed* and all kinds of wire on your estate or holding in any way, using where possible timber instead.

I remain, yours faithfully

W. Fitzherbert-Brockholes,
Hon. Sec., North Staff. Hunt.

## SMALLPOX

At the meeting of the Board of Guardians yesterday (Friday) it was decided, owing to the prevalence of small-pox at Willenhall, to suspend the visiting of friends of children in the Cottage Homes, Wednesfield, and also that no visitors be allowed at the workhouse until further orders. A discussion arose respecting the liability of the Willenhall Local Board to provide accommodation for pauper small-pox patients. The Clerk (Mr Pritchard) said that was the duty of the sanitary authorities, and unless something was done the County Council would probably build an isolation hospital for Willenhall, Wednesfield, and Heath Town, and charge the cost to those places.

*Staffordshire Advertiser May 12, 1894*

## A DISAGREEABLE GAME AT BURTON

On November 1st, Leek went away to play the Burton Rangers. The game was played on Messrs Bass and Co.'s ground, the long grass sadly hampering the players. There were only a few spectators, who could not understand that any team in Staffordshire, except it were a Burton team, knew how to play football. At half-time the game was equal, the Burton man who headed a goal for the homesters being clearly offside. Leek ultimately won a disagreeable game by three goals to one. On the same day the Leek 2nd string met Burslem Rangers at Leek, and won by thirteen goals to none, besides having two disallowed. The last goal of this match was scored by Jackson, the Leek goalkeeper, and of the others Shufflebotham scored five, Coates three, Goddard two, and Whittles two.

*Arthur Diehl*

BASS'S COOPERAGE, BURTON ON TRENT

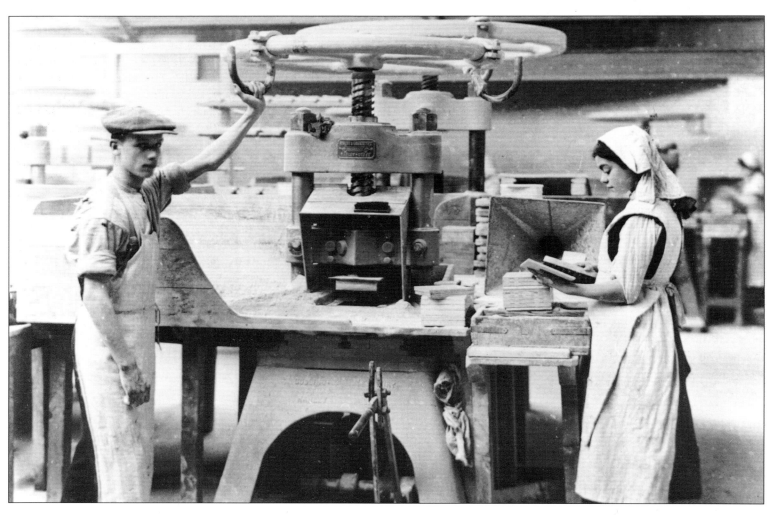

TILE MAKING IN THE POTTERIES

# Sources & Photographic Details

## TEXT

The page numbers given below relate to pages in this book and not to the page numbers in the source books.

The book sources are as follows: Alfred Barnard *Noted Breweries of Great Britain and Ireland* (1877) pp. 9, 38, 40, 84, 103; *Bass's Trip Book* (1911) p. 60; Arnold Bennett *Anna of the Five Towns* (1902) p. 19; *Clayhanger* (1910) p. 94; *Tales of the Five Towns* (1912) p. 63; C.J. Blagg *A History of the North Staffordshire Hounds and Country* (1902) p. 113; A. Diehl *Football in Leek* (1893) p. 113; George Heath *The Poems* (1870) p. 106; Alfred Hine *London, Leek, Macclesfield, The Potteries, Buxton, The Seasons, The Farmers' Calendar and other poems* (1897) p. 31; George Ewart Evans *Where Beards Wag All* (1970) pp. 52, 88, 91; *The Leek Annual* (1898) p. 105; *Midland Sketches* (1898) p. 49; W.H. Nithsdale *In The Highlands of Staffordshire* (1906) pp. 30, 50, 57, 102, 103; William Scarratt *Old Times in The Potteries* (1906) pp. 10, 33, 46, 49, 60; *Gipsy Smith: His Life and Work* (1903) p.11; *The Walfrunian (Wolverhampton School)* (1885) p. 15; *Walsall: Past and Present* (1905) p. 27; Alfred Williams *Sketches in and around Lichfield and Rugeley* (1892) pp. 47, 56.

Newspaper sources: *Daily Telegraph* p. 26; *Express and Star* pp. 81, 112; *Licensed Victualler's Gazette and Hotel Courier* p. 35; *Midland Evening News* p. 108; *Staffordshire Advertiser* pp. 34, 44, 82, 83, 84, 93, 113.

## ILLUSTRATIONS

The credits and notes on the illustrations used in the book are given in page ascending order. Sources are referred to by an abbreviation at the end of each entry and a key to these is given at the end of the section. When dates are known, or can reasonably be deduced, they are given and if the photographer is known the name follows in brackets.

Endpapers (front), Lichfield, distribution of traditional Bower cakes to children on Whit Monday, 1903 (Stone); BCL. Page i (half-title), Alexandrina van der Heydt and cousin, Robert Peel, at Drayton Manor near Tamworth, 1904 (Stone); BCL. Page ii, a family walk photographed near Hanley by an unknown amateur photographer, *c*. 1905; STM: Empire Theatre side-show at Lichfield Fair, *c*. 1900 (Stone); BCL.

Page iv (title), Webberly Street, Longton, *c*. 1900; WCK. Page v, departure of Bass's Trip from Burton Railway Station, 1911 (Simnett); GSY. Page 1, packing china in straw before crating for distribution, *c*. 1910; WCK. Page 2, the women's ward, Wolverhampton Union Workhouse, Bilston Road, *c*. 1900; WCL: Samuel Peploe Wood, sculptor, Great Haywood, 1890s; SMS. Page 3, Keele Hall, now part of Keele University, *c*. 1880; WCK. Page 4, a working day in the Potteries, *c*. 1910; WCK. Page 5, glazing plates in the Potteries, *c*. 1910; STM. Page 6, advertising postcard for Bass's Breweries, Burton on Trent, *c*. 1910; BMB. Page 7, inmates of St John's Hospital, Lichfield, 1900 (Stone); BCL. Page 8, advertisement for J. Withers & Son, spurs, bits, and stirrups makers, Wisemore Street, Walsall. This building now houses the Walsall Leather Centre and museum, WLC. Page 9, Queen Victoria's Jubilee celebrations, High Street, Burton on Trent, June 21, 1887; BMB. Page 10, distribution of soup to poor children, Burton on Trent, 1895 (Simnett); BMB. Page 11, Market Square, Tunstall, *c*. 1880; WCK. Page 12, Fountain Square, Hanley, 1880; WCK. Page 13, Lichfield market, 1900 (Stone); BCL: ice-cream barrow, Hanley, *c*. 1910; WCK. Page 14, rock dwellings, Kinver, 1893 (Stone); BCL. Page 15, bicycles (velocipedes) in a Staffordshire lane, *c*. 1900; WCK. Page 16, Lower Green and Mitre Inn, Tettenhall, 1890s; WCL. Page 17, Darlington Street, Wolverhampton, 1890s; WCL. Page 18, Alton village and castle, *c*. 1910; STM. Page 19, market and market-hall, Burton on Trent, *c*. 1900; BMB. Page 20, stacking saggars outside a bottle-oven, Longton, *c*. 1900; WCK. Page 21, making china dolls' heads, Longton, *c*. 1910; Wick. Page 22, railway bridge at Longton, *c*. 1910; STM: preparing clay using a hand-press, *c*. 1900; SMS. Page 23, casting cups in a hand-press mould using liquid clay, *c*. 1895; WCK. Page 25, hand-cranked potter's wheel, Longton, *c*. 1900; STM. Page 27, North Staffordshire railway, Stoke, 1890s; BJ. Page 28, J. Whitehouse, baker and confectioner, Walsall, *c*. 1910; WLHC. Page 29, butcher's shop, Cheadle, *c*. 1910; GS. Page 30, the Sheriff's Ride around the Lichfield city boundary, 1908 (Stone); BCL. Page 31, ox-roast·at Jubilee celebrations in Stapenhill, Burton on Trent, 1897 (Simnett); BMB. Page 32, Leek Grammar School, 1890s, RG. Page 33, loading stone onto a barge at Froghall Wharf for Sandbach, *c*. 1905; BJ. Page 34, market at Newcastle under Lyme, 1893; WCK. Page 35, delivery of domestic coal from New Haden Colliery, Town End, Cheadle, *c*. 1902; GS: opening of New Haden Colliery, Cheadle, 1902; SMS. Page 36, Worthington's Brewery, Burton on Trent, *c*. 1905; BMB: High Street,

Wolstanton, *c.* 1900; WCK. Page 37, Dudley Street, Wolverhampton, *c.* 1900; WCL. Page 38, Bass's hop store, Burton on Trent, 1890s (Keene); BMB. Page 39, Bass's barley store, Burton on Trent, 1890s (Keene); BMB. Page 40, Allsop's Brewery, Burton on Trent, *c.* 1910; BMB. Page 41, bride and groom, Rudyard *c.* 1910; BJ. Page 42, Staffs and Worcs Canal, Compton, near Wolverhampton, *c.* 1900; WCL. Page 43, farm labourers at Brook Farm, Perry Barr, 1900; (Stone); BCL: resident at cottage in Tutbury Castle, 1897 (Stone); BCL. Page 44, Henry Roden, Blacksmith, Penn, near Wolverhampton, 1890s; WCL. Page 45, Nellie Bass, daughter of Lord Bass, at Rangemore, the family home, near Burton on Trent, *c.* 1893; BMB. Page 46, Rushton village, *c.* 1900; JG. Page 47, horse fair at Rugeley, *c.* 1900; SMS. Page 48, market day in St Peter's Square, Wolverhampton, *c.* 1900; WCL. Page 49, Chubb's lock factory in the former workhouse building, *c.* 1913; WCL. Page 50, Staffs and Worcs Canal at Newbridge, *c.* 1900; WCL. Page 51, school group at Elford village school, 1903, (Stone); BCL. Page 52, Burton on Trent, *c.* 1900; BMB. Page 53, steam traction waggon, Bass, Ratcliff and Gretton's Burton on Trent, *c.* 1910; BMB: back-to-back houses, Longton, *c.* 1900; WCK. Page 54, Norfolk maltsters, 'Norkies', at Bass, Ratcliff and Gretton's, Burton on Trent, *c.* 1905; BMB. Page 55, opening of the Burton Tramways, August Bank Holiday, 1903; BMB. Page 56, village green, Abbot's Bromley, 1899 (Stone); BCL. page 57, Horn Dance, Abbot's Bromley, *c.* 1900 (Stone); BCL. Page 58, steam bus, Leek, *c.* 1904; RP. Page 59, the vegetable market, Wolverhampton, *c.* 1900; WCL. Page 60, horsefair in Leek, October 17, 1906 (Nithsdale); RP. Page 61, Bass's Brewery Trip to Yarmouth departing from Burton Station, 1909; BMB. Page 63, an unknown family outside their house in Burton on Trent, *c.* 1900; BMB. Page 64, group of town councillors from Darlaston, *c.* 1900; WLHC. Page 65, the Wedgwood Institute, Burslem, *c.* 1900; STM. Page 66, the Town Hall, Tunstall, *c.* 1905; STM. Page 67, funeral procession, Burslem, *c.* 1906; SMS: Town Hall, Burslem *c.* 1910; STM. Page 68, grocer and baker's cart, Hanley, *c.* 1900; STM. Page 69, hospital Saturday, Market Place, Uttoxeter, *c.* 1900; BJ: the Admiral Jervis Inn, Oakamoor, *c.* 1910; GS. Page 70, Market Day, Uttoxeter, *c.* 1905; SMS: Rollestone village, *c.* 1905; BMB. Page 71, David Brown, ironmonger, Brewood, *c.* 1910; SMS. Page 72, motorbus at Kingswinford, *c.* 1910; WSL. Page 73, Mulberry House, Hanley, *c.* 1890; WCK. Page 74, new grocery shop under construction, Shelton, *c.* 1900; WCK. Page 75, device for removing drunks from the Roebuck Inn, Trinity Street, Hanley, *c.* 1890; WCK. Page 76, the Edensor Hotel, Normacot, *c.* 1900; STM. Page 77, the Foaming Quart Inn, Burslem, *c.* 1880; WCK. Page 78, steam tram, Stoke, *c.* 1900; WCK. Page 79, school for children of The Cottage Homes, Wolverhampton, *c.* 1910; WCL. Page 80, lady in a gig, *c.* 1895; SMS. Page 81, Uttoxeter Market Place, 1904 (Stone); BCL. Page 82, Star Bank, Oakamoor with Thomas Bolton's cable factory in the background, *c.* 1910; GS: Cheadle Post Office, *c.* 1900; GS. Page 83, leather preparers at Wincer and Plant (purses and wallets), Walsall, *c.* 1906; WLC. Page 84, staff at A.A. Stubbs, horse collar makers, Lime Street, Walsall, *c.* 1910; WLC. Page 85, the old green Stapenhill, Burton on Trent,

*c.* 1905; RF: Bass's Brewery water tower, Burton on Trent, *c.* 1900; RF. Page 86, class at Tettenhall school, *c.* 1894; WSL. Page 87, cycle club, Burton on Trent, 1890s; RF: flower show at Burton on Trent, *c.* 1900; RF. Page 88, packing salt into sacks for butchers and fishmongers, Stafford, *c.* 1910; WSL: packing salt into drums for shop sale, *c.* 1910; WSL. Page 89, leather machinists at Wincer and Plant, Brixton Works, Glebe Street, Walsall (now Walsall Purse Co Ltd), *c.* 1906; WLC. Page 90, the new maltings at Wood Street, Burton on Trent, *c.* 1910; GSY: maltsters from East Anglia, called 'Norkies' by Burton people, *c.* 1910; GSY. Page 91, leisure time on the River Stour at Kinver, *c.* 1900; WSL. Page 92, Queen Street, Wolverhampton, *c.* 1900; WCL. Page 93, High House, Greengate Street, Stafford, *c.* 1900; WSL. Page 94, circus parade, High Street, Uttoxeter, *c.* 1900; UHC. Page 95, horse sale, Balance Street, Uttoxeter, *c.* 1900 (McCann); UHC: Guild Street, Burton on Trent, 1889 (Simnett); BMB. Page 96, the ford at Forsbrook, *c.* 1900; WCK: fishing at Dimmingsdale, near Cheadle, 1890s; WCK. Page 97, steam-driven tram at Stoke, *c.* 1895; WCK: young man, Rudyard *c.* 1900; BJ. Page 98, making crates for packing china, *c.* 1895; WCK: back-to-back houses in the Potteries, *c.* 1900; STM. Page 99, the Clarion Club, Hanley, *c.* 1905; STM. Page 100, Arnold Bennett, novelist, with family and servants at home, Waterloo Road, Cobridge, *c.* 1890. Page 101, factory girls wearing clogs, a picture used as a lecture slide by Staffordshire Public Health Department in attempts to improve awareness of the need for improvements in living and working conditions. *c* 1910; SMS: amateur photographer's family in Hanley Park, *c.* 1910; STM. Page 102, men decorating china in the Potteries, 1890s; STM. Page 103, girls' cookery class, board school, Longton, *c.* 1900; WCK. Page 104, procession in Leek for Coronation celebrations, June 2, 1911; RP. Page 105, Manifold Valley Railway train, *c.* 1910; BJ. Page 106, boating on Rudyard Lake, near Leek, *c.* 1910; RP. Page 107, haymaking at Compton Farm, Compton, *c.* 1900; WCL. Page 108, laundry lessons, Royal School Orphanage, Wolverhampton, *c.* 1900; SMS. Pge 109, music lessons, Royal School Orphanage, Wolverhampton, *c.* 1900; SMS. Page 110, washday in Longnor, *c.* 1900; SMS. Page 111, pawnbroker's shop, Burslem, *c.* 1905; STM: stall-holders at Uttoxeter market, *c.* 1900; SMS. Page 112, childrens' ward, Wolverhampton Union Workhouse, Bilston Road, *c.* 1900; WCL. Page 113, the drying yard, Stafford Laundry, *c.* 1906; SMS. Page 114, pyramid stacks of casks at Bass's Brewery, Burton on Trent, 1890s (Keene); BMB: tile-making in the Potteries, using powdered clay, *c.* 1910; WCK. Endpapers (back), market-day, St Peter's Square, Wolverhampton, *c.* 1900; WCL.

Key: BMB, Bass Museum, Burton on Trent. BCL, Birmingham Central Library. RF, Richard Farman. BJ, Basil Jeuda. RP, Ray Poole. WSL, William Salt Library, Stafford, GS, George Short. GSY, Geoffrey Sowerby. STM, Stoke on Trent Museum and Art Gallery. SMS, Staffordshire Museum Service, Shugborough. UHC, Uttoxeter Heritage Centre. WLC, Walsall Leather Centre. WLHC, Walsall Local History Centre. WCK, Warrillow Collection, Keele University. WCL, Wolverhampton Central Library.